Ethnic and Indigenous Business Studies

In mainstream society, an automobile is understood to be a personally owned asset. In parts of New Caledonia, a private vehicle has a cultural liability in that it is socially incorrect to use a car solely for personal benefit. This is somewhat like the situation in Lesotho where a privately-owned cow cannot be sold nor killed by its owner. Among Indigenous Basuto people, the proprietor of cattle has the obligation to allow others to use cows for transport or other uses.

Cultural assumptions, whether explicit or implicit, are often ignored or misunderstood, yet central to understanding business. The purpose of this series is to bring light to business as conducted by ethnic minorities and indigenous peoples, with an emphasis on understanding the cultural behaviors that shape specific economic structures. This is an interdisciplinary book series welcoming all approaches to research on ethnic and indigenous business origins, practices, history, evolution, demographics, and challenges. Academic monographs, edited volumes, and case studies are welcome. Ultimately, the series aims to provide a nuanced perspective of mainstream business thought, and usher in a spirit of inclusion to a mature understanding of business philosophies.

Hajer Jarrar · Léo-Paul Dana · Virginie Hachard ·
George Lodorfos
Editors

Diaspora Angel Investing

Global Networks, Local Impact

Springer

Editors
Hajer Jarrar
Excelia Business School
La Rochelle, France

Léo-Paul Dana
Kazimieras Simonavicius University
Vilnuis, Lithuania

Virginie Hachard
EM Normandie Business School
Le Havre, France

George Lodorfos
Leeds Business School
Leeds, UK

ISSN 2948-1635 ISSN 2948-1643 (electronic)
Ethnic and Indigenous Business Studies
ISBN 978-3-032-33087-1 ISBN 978-3-032-33088-8 (eBook)
https://doi.org/10.1007/978-3-032-33088-8

This Springer imprint is published by the registered company Springer Nature Switzerland AG
The registered company address is: Gewerbestrasse 11, 6330 Cham, Switzerland

Book Disclaimer on Photographic Content Involving Human Subjects

This publication contains photographic material featuring individuals and communities involved in social science research. All images are included solely for scholarly, educational, and non-commercial purposes. Informed consent was obtained from all identifiable individuals depicted, with full disclosure of the context, purpose, and potential dissemination of this work. Where appropriate, additional permissions were secured from legal guardians, community leaders, or cultural authorities, particularly in the case of vulnerable or indigenous populations.

The author and publisher have taken all reasonable measures to ensure that the dignity, privacy, and cultural values of those represented are respected. Identifiable information has been anonymized where necessary, and no image has been included that could reasonably be expected to cause harm, distress, or misrepresentation.

The use of these images complies with institutional ethical review protocols and adheres to internationally recognized standards, including the Declaration of Helsinki and the Singapore Statement on Research Integrity.

Contents

Contributors

Razan Al-Masri Entrepreneurship and Innovation Centre, Abu Dhabi School of Management, Abu Dhabi, United Arab Emirates

Eiman Ashraf City University Ajman, Ajman, United Arab Emirates

Marc Audi Entrepreneurship and Innovation Centre, Abu Dhabi School of Management, Abu Dhabi, United Arab Emirates

Nada Mallah Boustani Saint Joseph University of Beirut, Beirut, Lebanon

Tehreem Fatima University of Sargodha, Sargodha, Pakistan

Sanaa Hajj Safa LIRSA Laboratory-Cnam, Paris, France

L.' Hocine Houanti EM Normandie Business School, Le Havre, France

Gozde Inal Cavlan Department of Business Administration, Altinbas Cyprus University, Nicosia-Cyprus, Turkey

Roy Matta USJ Business School, Saint Joseph University of Beirut, Beirut, Lebanon

Hani Mawlawi East International University, Tripoly, Lebanon

Guido Migliaccio Department of Law, Economics, Management and Quantitative Methods (DEMM), University of Sannio, Benevento, Italy

Marion Polge USJ Business School, Saint Joseph University of Beirut, Beirut, Lebanon

Marc Poulin Entrepreneurship & Innovation Centre, Abu Dhabi School of Management, Abu Dhabi, United Arab Emirates

Matteo Rossi University of Sannio, Benevento, Italy

Jean-Michel Sahut IDRAC Business School, Lyon, France

Charbel Salloum Métis Lab, EM Normandie Business School, Clichy, France

Muhammad Saleem Sumbal Department of Industrial and Systems Engineering, The Hong Kong Polytechnic University, Hong Kong, China

Ali Tariq Management Science, Unviersity of Lahore, Sargodha, Pakistan

Divya Upadhyay Entrepreneurship & Innovation Centre, Abu Dhabi School of Management, Abu Dhabi, United Arab Emirates

Constance Van Horne Entrepreneurship and Innovation Centre, Abu Dhabi School of Management, Abu Dhabi, United Arab Emirates

Ruba Younes USJ Business School, Saint Joseph University of Beirut, Beirut, Lebanon

Nadia Zahoor School of Business and Management, Queen Mary University of London, London, UK;
Innolab, University of Vaasa, Vaasa, Finland;
Department of Management and Marketing, King Fahd University of Petroleum and Minerals, Dhahran, Saudi Arabia

From Kinship to Capital

Charbel Salloum

Abstract This chapter explains why diaspora angels have become strategically important in early-stage finance, especially where domestic capital markets remain shallow and formal venture intermediation is weak. It does not treat diaspora investors as a sentimental category or as a substitute for professional investing. Instead, it synthesizes mature evidence on what makes diaspora angels distinctive: they can lower search costs, interpret local context for foreign capital, transfer trust across borders, and help ventures move from community credibility to market credibility. The chapter also clarifies where those advantages are strongest and where they are commonly overstated. Drawing on research on diaspora entrepreneurship, cross-border angel finance, and diaspora policy, it argues that diaspora angels add the most value when identity-based access is combined with disciplined screening, credible governance, and realistic follow-on pathways. The result is a clearer explanation of why diaspora angels matter and how they should be positioned in an investable ecosystem.

1 Introduction

Diaspora angel investing often begins before any term sheet appears. A founder is introduced by a cousin, a university alumnus, a regional association, or a respected professional abroad. That origin can make the phenomenon look informal or purely relational. The better reading is more demanding. Diaspora angels matter because they sit at the point where identity-based access meets investment judgment. They can see ventures that conventional financiers struggle to see, not simply because they care, but because they can interpret signals that would otherwise remain opaque (Leblang, 2010; Riddle et al., 2010; Brinkerhoff, 2012).

This is especially important in markets where the financing chain is broken. Many young firms sit above the level of family funding and below the ticket size or risk tolerance of institutional venture capital. In such settings, the first investor is rarely

C. Salloum (✉)
Métis Lab, EM Normandie Business School, Clichy, France
e-mail: csalloum@em-normandie.fr

H. Jarrar et al. (eds.), *Diaspora Angel Investing*, Ethnic and Indigenous Business Studies, https://doi.org/10.1007/978-3-032-33088-8_1

just a capital provider. That investor is also a translator of uncertainty, a validator of founder quality, and a bridge between local opportunity and external standards. Research on angel markets across countries shows that early stage investing is highly sensitive to institutions, investor capabilities, and cross national distance, which makes the role of bridge actors unusually valuable (Li & Zahra, 2012; Cumming & Zhang, 2019).

Diaspora angels are often described as automatically superior to domestic angels or foreign venture capitalists. The literature does not support that kind of romance. Identity can open doors, but it can also distort judgment. What makes diaspora angels distinctive is not emotional attachment by itself. Their advantage lies in dual embeddedness. They can understand the social texture of a home market while still recognizing what outside investors, customers, and later stage financiers need to see before a company becomes broadly investable (Tong, 2005; Ragazzi, 2014; Dizo-Conteh et al., 2025).

This chapter takes that more disciplined view. It explains why diaspora angels emerge where they do, what they contribute beyond money, where their involvement is most credible, and what conditions make their participation effective rather than merely symbolic. The argument is deliberately mature. It does not propose a new model. Instead, it consolidates what the evidence already shows about diaspora finance when kinship based access is converted into commercial capital.

A useful starting correction is to separate diaspora angel investing from remittances, donations, and ceremonial engagement. Remittances stabilize household welfare. Philanthropy may support schools, clinics, or community projects. Angel investing does something different. It prices uncertainty, accepts the possibility of loss, and expects commercial discipline in return for upside. That distinction matters because states and founders often approach diaspora capital with a language of belonging, while investors must ultimately decide with a language of risk, governance, and scalability. The diaspora policy literature has long warned that emotional attachment is a resource only when institutions make participation practical (Brinkerhoff, 2012; Ragazzi, 2014; Park, 2021).

Once that distinction is made, the real contribution of diaspora angels becomes clearer. They are not valuable because they care more in the abstract. They are valuable because they can connect three things that rarely meet smoothly at the seed stage: local opportunity, external standards, and enough confidence to write the first serious check. In corridors where ethnic, educational, or professional ties already support cross-border trade and investment, that bridging role can be unusually strong. The relevant mechanism is not sentiment alone, but the way familiarity lowers search cost and helps investors interpret signals that would otherwise remain noisy or invisible (Tong, 2005; Leblang, 2010; Dizo-Conteh et al., 2025).

2 Why Diaspora Angels Emerge where Finance Chains Are Thin

The first reason diaspora angels matter is structural. Early-stage finance is full of search and screening problems, even in deep markets. In thinner markets, those frictions become sharper because founders have fewer visible comparables, fewer intermediaries, and weaker routes into trusted investor networks. Diaspora actors can reduce those frictions at the front end of the market by bringing deal flow into view. Their social and professional ties create access to founders, sectors, and places that outsiders would find costly to reach or difficult to interpret (Riddle et al., 2010; Brinkerhoff, 2012; Cumming & Zhang, 2019).

Importantly, diaspora angels do not solve scarcity by replacing institutions. They make weak markets more navigable by lowering the cost of first contact and first conviction. A founder who would look unverified to a distant investor may look legitimate to someone who understands the school system, industry reputation, family business background, or home region of the entrepreneur. That kind of familiarity does not eliminate risk, yet it can help investors decide which opportunities deserve professional diligence rather than immediate dismissal (Leblang, 2010; Park, 2021).

A second structural factor is corridor formation. Diaspora investment does not move evenly across countries. It tends to cluster in pathways where migration history, commercial exchange, and professional mobility have already built channels of communication. Those channels matter because they reduce the number of interpretive jumps between founder and funder. Research on diaspora entrepreneurship consistently shows that cross border economic activity is easier to sustain when actors can work across home and host institutions rather than being trapped in one of them (Ojo et al., 2013; Schmutzler et al., 2021).

This is why diaspora angels often appear before formal funds do. Angel investing can tolerate smaller deals, imperfect information, and higher involvement. That makes it a practical starting point for equity mobilization in corridors where opportunities are promising but the market is not yet thick enough for scaled venture capital. The logic is not patriotic charity. It is micro market formation. Small groups of informed investors can test whether a corridor has repeatable deals, credible founders, and enough follow on potential to justify more organized capital later (Lerner et al., 2018; Mason et al., 2022).

Seen in that light, kinship is not the endpoint. It is the opening mechanism. Diaspora angels matter because they can move ventures from a world of private recognition into a world of investable evidence. That transition is difficult, but it is exactly where early stage ecosystems either deepen or stall.

This is one reason diaspora angels repeatedly show up in settings where the formal financing ladder is incomplete rather than absent. India offers the clearest large-scale illustration. Diaspora participation mattered not simply because nonresident investors had money, but because they could identify exportable businesses and connect them to international standards at a time when domestic intermediation was still maturing. In African and Balkan contexts, the pattern is similar even at smaller scales. Returnees and diaspora professionals often help founders cross the first credibility threshold by bringing outside expectations into local ventures and local context into outside conversations (Tong, 2005; Leblang, 2010; Nyame-Asiamah et al., 2020; Mustafa, 2021; Schmutzler et al., 2021).

The economics of the first check also matter. Many promising ventures require ticket sizes that are too large for family finance and too small or too risky for formal venture funds. Diaspora angels can operate in that gap because angel investing tolerates imperfect information and rewards close involvement. That does not make the asset class easy. It means the investor can profit from doing work that institutions find too expensive at small scale. International evidence on angel markets and cross-border business angel activity shows that such investors are especially valuable when they can combine hands-on judgment with syndication and later-stage pathway building, rather than acting as isolated benefactors (Lerner et al., 2018; Cumming & Zhang, 2019; Mason et al., 2022).

Equally important, diaspora angels often emerge before a corridor becomes legible to outsiders because they can bear ambiguity at the exploration stage. They know which sectors are culturally overhyped, which local success stories are mostly narrative, and which founder reputations actually carry weight across professional communities. That ability to discriminate early between noise and opportunity is hard to institutionalize quickly. It is one reason corridor formation often begins with individuals and networks before it is noticed by funds, accelerators, or public agencies.

3 What Diaspora Angels Add beyond Money

Capital is only one part of the contribution. The more distinctive the value, the more it often lies in interpretation. Diaspora angels can help founders present the business in a language that travels. They know when a locally impressive achievement will mean little abroad, and they know which signals will actually travel across borders, such as verified customer revenue, regulatory clarity, export readiness, or a founder profile that can stand up in an international data room (Riddle et al., 2010; Mason et al., 2022; Dizo-Conteh et al., 2025).

They also transfer trust, though not in a simplistic way. In many diaspora deals, the initial introduction comes from a person whose reputation substitutes for the institutional certainty that is missing. That reputation does not guarantee the venture's quality. What it does is reduce the probability that the opportunity is wholly spurious. In practice, that helps investors decide where to spend diligence time. Research on diaspora networks and entrepreneurial ecosystems suggests that this trust transfer is one of the mechanisms through which diaspora actors help overcome institutional distance (Brinkerhoff, 2012; Schmutzler et al., 2021).

Another contribution is commercial reach. Diaspora angels often have direct knowledge of customer needs, procurement norms, compliance expectations, and partnership cultures in host markets. That matters greatly for young ventures because export potential is not created by aspiration alone. It depends on knowing which product features, certifications, channels, or proof points matter in the target market. Studies of diaspora-backed internationalization show that these networks can move firms from local relevance to cross-border commercial traction faster than firms could manage on their own (Dizo-Conteh et al., 2025).

There is also a governance effect. Experienced diaspora angels often push founders toward cleaner cap tables, more disciplined reporting, and more realistic milestone planning. Those interventions may seem modest, yet they change the future financeability of the company. A venture that learns early to separate relationship warmth from governance discipline is much easier to syndicate, easier to diligence, and easier to position for a future lead investor (Edelman et al., 2017; Cumming & Zhang, 2019).

Still, value added is not automatic. Recent evidence on diaspora investment motives shows that financial and emotional social drivers can coexist in the same decision, which is precisely why discipline matters. Identity may accelerate engagement, but it should not create a valuation premium of its own. The strongest diaspora angels treat community proximity as an informational asset, not as a substitute for price discipline or legal clarity (Park, 2021; Park & Tuxhorn, 2025).

The translation function is more demanding than it first appears. Founders frequently assume that a strong local reputation or a compelling social mission will speak for itself abroad. It rarely does. Diaspora angels help by converting diffuse credibility into portable proof. They push entrepreneurs to specify customer acquisition, regulatory status, gross margin logic, and reporting rhythm in forms that can survive outside the home network. In this sense, trust is useful because it motivates closer scrutiny, not because it excuses the absence of evidence. Work on diaspora entrepreneurship, angel investing, and investor signaling reaches the same practical point from different angles: identity may open the file, but financeability depends on what can be verified and repeated (Riddle et al., 2010; Edelman et al., 2017; Park & Tuxhorn, 2025).

Another advantage is that diaspora angels often know what cross border commercial traction actually looks like. They have seen which certifications buyers insist on, how enterprise procurement differs from home-market selling, where channel partners create leverage, and what kinds of compliance weakness will later block growth. That is why their advice can matter as much as their money. A founder may discover, for example, that the venture's true bottleneck is not demand but payment processing, data governance, or documentation discipline. Investors who understand both sides of the corridor can identify those bottlenecks earlier and connect the venture to the right professional service providers, reference customers, or pilot opportunities (Brinkerhoff, 2012; Dizo-Conteh et al., 2025; Kontakos & Stavrou, 2025).

Finally, diaspora angels frequently improve a firm's readiness for syndication. Early governance habits travel forward. A company that learns to maintain a clean cap table, document board decisions, and report against clear milestones is easier to back in the next round. This is where value added becomes cumulative. The original diaspora investor is not merely supporting the founder in a moment of scarcity. The investor is helping create an asset that can be evaluated by others who do not share the same relationship network. Table 1 summarizes the mechanisms, risks, and better practices associated with that transition.

Table 1 What makes diaspora angels distinctive and where the advantage can fail

Mechanism	Why it matters	Main risk	Better practice
Kinship and community access	Lowers search costs and reveals founders before formal intermediaries do	Warm introductions are mistaken for investment quality	Treat social access as a sourcing advantage, not as a diligence shortcut
Dual embeddedness	Helps investors translate local context for outside capital and markets	Context is overinterpreted and risks are normalized	Convert local knowledge into verifiable evidence that other investors can inspect
Trust transfer	Makes first meetings and first checks more likely	Community endorsement crowds out independent verification	Use trusted intermediaries to prioritize deals, then verify commercially and legally
Cross border reach	Supports customer access, hiring, and follow on introductions abroad	Founders overstate export readiness or network strength	Link capital to concrete milestones such as pilots, contracts, or regulatory clearance
Identity based commitment	Can increase patience and engagement in difficult markets	Sentiment weakens valuation and governance discipline	Separate mission from pricing, terms, and reporting requirements
Commercial reach	Connects ventures to customer expectations, certifications, and distribution norms in host markets	Internationalisation remains aspirational and untested	Ask for named routes to market, reference customers, and proof that the host market logic is specific rather than rhetorical
Governance transfer	Introduces cleaner reporting, cap tables, and milestone discipline before institutional capital arrives	Relationship warmth delays difficult governance conversations	Use standard documents, information rights, and explicit conditions for follow on funding
Syndication bridge	Makes locally credible ventures legible to outside angels and later funds	Deals stay trapped inside one community circle	Pair corridor insiders with sector, legal, or lead investors who can validate and price risk independently

Source Author's own elaboration based on Leblang (2010), Riddle et al. (2010), Brinkerhoff (2012), Park (2021), Mason et al. (2022), and Dizo-Conteh et al. (2025)

The table also suggests why diaspora angels should be considered corridor specialists rather than simply investors with a cultural connection. Their real edge appears when they can combine access, translation, and post-investment discipline in the same deal. A warm relationship without commercial reach is not enough. Market knowledge without the transfer of governance is not enough either. The strongest cases arise when the investor can help the venture become legible to the next counterpart, whether that is a customer abroad, a co-investor, or a later-stage fund.

This is also why organized diaspora groups can outperform isolated individuals. Groups widen sourcing, reduce dependence on a single community gatekeeper, and make it easier to split labor among screening, diligence, and mentoring. They are more likely to spot when a founder is genuinely exceptional but socially peripheral, which matters because the most investable venture in a corridor is not always the most visible one. Professionalization, therefore, broadens opportunity as much as it reduces risk.

4 Where Diaspora Angels Fit Best

Diaspora angel capital is most credible where ventures can translate local insight into products or services that travel. Border crossing software, business services, health-related platforms, specialist manufacturing, and climate-enabling solutions often fit this pattern better than ventures whose economics depend entirely on a narrowly local demand base. The core issue is not glamour. It is portability. A deal becomes more investable when customers, talent, distribution, or exit options can be connected across corridors rather than trapped in a single institutionally thin market (Lerner et al., 2018; Mason et al., 2022).

The Indian experience illustrates this point well. As the entrepreneurial finance ecosystem deepened, diaspora-backed companies could more readily move from angel capital to larger rounds because there was a more visible finance escalator and a larger population of knowledgeable investors. The lesson is not that every country should mechanically imitate India. It is that diaspora angels are strongest where they sit within a capital chain rather than carrying the whole chain themselves (Mustafa, 2021).

Other corridors teach a different lesson. Evidence from South African entrepreneurs and European business angels shows how much cross-border deals depend on signaling and interpretation. The problem is rarely an absolute absence of opportunity. More often, it is the gap between what founders know locally and what foreign investors can verify credibly. Diaspora and bridge investors become valuable precisely because they can narrow that gap without pretending that it has disappeared (Hain et al., 2016; Mestwerdt et al., 2025).

Balkan and African returnee settings add further nuance. In those environments, diaspora actors often help create opportunity-driven ecosystems by linking local ventures to professional norms, market information, and commercial pathways abroad. At the same time, the evidence shows that the decision to invest depends on institutional conditions at home as much as on emotional attachment. Return is not crowded out by identity. Rather, the two are negotiated together, which means corridor quality remains central (Nyame-Asiamah et al., 2020; Schmutzler et al., 2021).

A final reminder comes from corridors that are more gateway-oriented than startup-oriented. Research on Israeli and Jewish diaspora investment in Cyprus, for instance, highlights how some diaspora channels are especially attractive for holding structures, services, gateway positioning, and broader FDI logic. In those settings, an early-stage angel lens may capture only part of the opportunity. The mature investor asks which vehicle best fits the corridor, rather than forcing every diaspora relationship into a startup equity format (Kontakos & Stavrou, 2025).

This helps explain why some sectors repeatedly attract diaspora angels, while others remain difficult to attract. Ventures selling to fragmented local consumers can certainly succeed, but they are harder to evaluate across borders when the investor cannot observe the market directly and when later capital is scarce. By contrast, exportable software, business services, specialist manufacturing, health technologies, and climate-enabling products often produce clearer cross-border logic. Their milestones can be described in terms of travel, and their customer pathways are more compatible with diaspora commercial knowledge. The criterion is not whether a venture sounds innovative. It is whether the corridor gives the investor a practical informational edge.

Country examples reinforce that point. In India, the maturation of startup finance made it easier for diaspora angels to operate within a recognizable escalator from seed to growth capital. In Balkan economies, diaspora and returnee investors have often been most useful where they connect local founders to wider entrepreneurial ecosystems and professional norms rather than acting as perpetual substitute capital. In gateway economies such as Cyprus, diaspora-linked investment may enter through structures or sectors that make more sense as regional access plays than as conventional startup stories. The lesson is to let corridor economics determine the right investment form, rather than forcing every opportunity into a single angel template (Mustafa, 2021; Schmutzler et al., 2021; Kontakos & Stavrou, 2025).

The negative case is equally revealing. Diaspora angels tend to struggle when they are expected to solve problems that are fundamentally infrastructural. If contract enforcement is unreliable, if foreign exchange rules make repatriation opaque, or if no credible path exists for capital or acquisitions, corridor familiarity can only do so much. Mature investors, therefore, ask a harder question than whether the founder is strong. They ask whether the corridor can support repetition. Without that, the deal may still be worthy, but it belongs in a different risk bucket and should be priced and structured accordingly (Cumming & Zhang, 2019; Mason et al., 2022).

5 What Can Go Wrong and What Good Practice Looks like

The most common mistake is to confuse access with investability. A warm introduction can create momentum, but momentum is not evidence. When diaspora angels skip basic diligence because the founder is known to the community, the very feature that opened the deal can later damage it. Informality may expedite the initial check, yet it can weaken follow-on financing if later investors encounter opaque accounts, undocumented shareholder rights, or a cap table shaped by goodwill rather than governance (Riddle et al., 2010; Park & Tuxhorn, 2025).

Network concentration is another risk. Diaspora investment circles are often tight, which helps trust formation but can also create blind spots. The same gatekeepers may repeatedly fund familiar founder profiles, sectors, or regions while overlooking less connected but stronger opportunities. Over time, that can narrow rather than widen the entrepreneurial pipeline. Mature ecosystems counter this by professionalizing screening, widening sourcing channels, and syndicating beyond the immediate community when appropriate (Edelman et al., 2017; Cumming & Zhang, 2019).

The third risk is strategic overreach. Diaspora angels are sometimes asked to finance ventures in corridors where later capital, legal enforceability, and plausible exits remain too weak. That is not a reason to retreat from difficult markets. It is a reason to size exposure correctly and to choose sectors whose business models can travel. If a corridor cannot support later funding or acquisition interest, a stronger identity alone does not solve the problem. It has to be addressed through structure, syndication, or a different instrument entirely (Lerner et al., 2018; Mason et al., 2022).

Policy design also matters. Governments often celebrate diaspora finance with outreach campaigns, symbolic recognition, or special engagement offices. Those moves may help, but the literature is consistent on a deeper point. Diaspora investment expands when the environment becomes commercially usable. That means contract enforcement, tax clarity, disclosure standards, credible intermediaries, and fewer frictions in moving and monitoring capital. Symbolism without implementation rarely changes investor behavior for long (Brinkerhoff, 2012; Ragazzi, 2014; Park, 2021).

Good practice, therefore, looks surprisingly unsentimental. The best diaspora angels preserve the advantages of familiarity while building habits associated with professional investing: clear screening criteria, structured diligence, realistic valuation, milestone-based follow-on funding, and syndication where local or sector expertise is needed. In that form, diaspora capital becomes less a romantic exception and more a disciplined bridge from local promise to scalable finance (Dizo-Conteh et al., 2025; Park & Tuxhorn, 2025).

This is where professional routines become decisive. The best diaspora angels create a discipline that preserves the advantages of familiarity rather than eroding them. They document why the opportunity is compelling, which claims have been verified, what would invalidate the thesis, and which milestones should trigger additional capital. They also bring complementary expertise when the corridor connection is insufficient. Sector specialists, local counsel, accountants, and co-investors widen the field of vision and reduce the chance that one trusted relationship defines the whole investment case. Those habits are consistent with the broader evidence on angel learning, valuation discipline, and the role of syndication in improving investment judgment (Edelman et al., 2017; Lerner et al., 2018; Mason et al., 2022).

Public policy can either reinforce or weaken those routines. Outreach offices, diaspora registries, and celebratory narratives may enhance visibility, but they do not substitute for tax clarity, enforceable contracts, credible intermediaries, or a reasonable route for moving capital. The diaspora policy literature is remarkably consistent on this point. Investors respond to environments that reduce transaction friction and protect commercial seriousness. When governments treat diaspora capital primarily as a patriotic resource, they often raise expectations while leaving the actual investment process cumbersome and uncertain (Brinkerhoff, 2012; Ragazzi, 2014; Park, 2021).

Good practice, therefore, looks less heroic and more repeatable. Source broadly, diligence hard, structure clearly, and keep the company financeable for the next investor. When corridor familiarity is combined with those routines, diaspora angels do more than fill a funding gap. They help build the norms that make a market investable to a wider circle of capital.

A final sign of maturity is that the investor defines success in portfolio rather than anecdotal terms. One celebrated diaspora-backed exit can create attention, but a functioning market requires repeat founders, cleaner follow-on rounds, and a broader set of ventures entering the pipeline with investable records. Angels who understand this do not merely ask whether a single company can win. They ask whether their investment habits are helping the corridor produce a second, third, and fourth financeable company over time.

6 Conclusion

Diaspora angels matter because they can do work that ordinary capital often cannot do well at the earliest stage. They can see opportunities through social and professional channels that are invisible to outsiders, translate local credibility into investable signals, and connect ventures to markets and standards beyond the home country. In thin financing environments, those functions are consequential rather than decorative.

At the same time, the evidence points toward a disciplined conclusion. Diaspora angels are most valuable when they institutionalize the advantages of familiarity instead of being captured by them. The path from kinship to capital is strongest when access is followed by verification, when identity is followed by governance, and when initial within capital is positioned inside a realistic corridor for follow-on finance. That is why diaspora angels deserve a central place in the early-stage financing conversation, but only as a professional bridge rather than a sentimental exception.

That is also why diaspora angel investing deserves to be taken seriously as part of entrepreneurial finance rather than left inside the softer language of community support. At its best, it converts proximity into better selection, better preparation, and better market access. At its weakest, it confuses social endorsement with commercial proof. The difference lies in whether familiarity is organized into a process that other investors can respect and eventually join.

For founders, the strategic implication is equally clear. The most productive use of diaspora capital is not to court it as forgiving money, but to use it as demanding bridge capital. Founders who arrive with cleaner documentation, sharper customer evidence, and a more explicit plan for how the venture becomes legible to outsiders make far better use of the diaspora advantage. In that setting, community proximity does not dilute standards. It increases the likelihood that high standards can be achieved earlier and at a lower relational cost.

For policymakers and ecosystem builders, the deeper lesson is that diaspora angels are most effective when they can operate inside a recognizable escalator of finance, expertise, and legal reliability. Where that escalator is missing, the angel's role becomes heavier and more fragile. Where it exists, diaspora investors can specialize in what they do best: sourcing overlooked opportunities, interpreting corridor realities, and helping ventures cross the line from trusted locally to financeable internationally.

References

Brinkerhoff, J. M. (2012). Creating an enabling environment for diasporas' participation in homeland development. *International Migration, 50*(1), 75–95. https://doi.org/10.1111/j.1468-2435.2009.00542.x

Cumming, D., & Zhang, M. (2019). Angel investors around the world. *Journal of International Business Studies, 50*(5), 692–719. https://doi.org/10.1057/s41267-018-0178-0

Dizo-Conteh, U., Tasavori, M., & Afrahi, B. (2025). The contribution of diaspora networks to the internationalisation of SMEs: A case study in the healthcare industry. *Journal of International Management, 31*(6), 101306. https://doi.org/10.1016/j.intman.2025.101306

Edelman, L. F., Manolova, T. S., & Brush, C. G. (2017). Angel investing: A literature review. *Foundations and Trends in Entrepreneurship, 13*(4–5), 265–439. https://doi.org/10.1561/0300000051

Hain, D., Johan, S., & Wang, D. (2016). Determinants of cross-border venture capital investments in emerging and developed economies: The effects of relational and institutional trust. *Journal of Business Ethics, 138*(4), 743–764. https://doi.org/10.1007/s10551-015-2772-4

Kontakos, P., & Stavrou, S. (2025). Israeli and Jewish diaspora investment in Cyprus: FDI determinants, entry modes, and institutional challenges. *Journal of East-West Business. Advance online publication.* https://doi.org/10.1080/10669868.2025.2595351

Leblang, D. (2010). Familiarity breeds investment: Diaspora networks and international investment. *American Political Science Review, 104*(3), 584–600. https://doi.org/10.1017/S0003055410000201

Lerner, J., Schoar, A., Sokolinski, S., & Wilson, K. (2018). The globalization of angel investments: Evidence across countries. *Journal of Financial Economics, 127*(1), 1–20. https://doi.org/10.1016/j.jfineco.2017.05.012

Mason, C., Botelho, T., & Duggett, J. (2022). Promoting cross-border investing by business angels in the European Union. *Regional Studies, 56*(8), 1391–1403. https://doi.org/10.1080/00343404.2021.1960961

Mustafa, M. (2021). Angel investing: The untold story of India. *Palgrave Macmillan.* https://doi.org/10.1007/978-981-16-0921-3

Nyame-Asiamah, F., Amoako, I. O., Amankwah-Amoah, J., & Debrah, Y. A. (2020). Diaspora entrepreneurs' push and pull institutional factors for investing in Africa: Insights from African returnees from the United Kingdom. *Technological Forecasting and Social Change, 152*, 119876. https://doi.org/10.1016/j.techfore.2019.119876

Ojo, S., Nwankwo, S., & Gbadamosi, A. (2013). African diaspora entrepreneurs: Navigating entrepreneurial spaces in 'home' and 'host' countries. *International Journal of Entrepreneurship and Innovation, 14*(4), 289–299. https://doi.org/10.5367/ijei.2013.0126

Park, S. B. (2021). Courting foreign direct investment from diasporas: Are diaspora engagement policies effective? Under what conditions? *Pacific Focus, 36*(2), 252–286. https://doi.org/10.1111/pafo.12188

Park, S., & Tuxhorn, K.-L. (2025). Investment across borders: How diaspora firms weigh financial returns and emotional-social drivers. *Asian and Pacific Migration Journal, 34*(4), 653–675. https://doi.org/10.1177/01171968251393548

Ragazzi, F. (2014). A comparative analysis of diaspora policies. *Political Geography, 41*, 74–89. https://doi.org/10.1016/j.polgeo.2013.12.004

Riddle, L., Hrivnak, G. A., & Nielsen, T. M. (2010). Transnational diaspora entrepreneurship in emerging markets: Bridging institutional divides. *Journal of International Management, 16*(4), 398–411. https://doi.org/10.1016/j.intman.2010.09.009

Schmutzler, J., Andonova, V., & Perez-Lopez, J. (2021). The role of diaspora in opportunity-driven entrepreneurial ecosystems: A mixed-methods study of Balkan economies. *International Entrepreneurship and Management Journal, 17*(2), 693–729. https://doi.org/10.1007/s11365-020-00708-4

Tong, S. Y. (2005). Ethnic networks in FDI and the impact of institutional development. *Review of Development Economics, 9*(4), 563–580. https://doi.org/10.1111/j.1467-9361.2005.00294.x

Diaspora Angels as Pipeline Builders: Community Hubs, Accelerators, and Platforms in Emerging Ecosystems

Sanaa Hajj Safa, Nada Mallah Boustani, and Hani Mawlawi

Abstract This chapter two examines the role of diaspora actors as pipeline builders within entrepreneurial ecosystems in emerging and fragile contexts. It focuses on how transnational networks contribute to entrepreneurship through funding, knowledge transfer, and legitimacy building. In crisis-affected environments such as Lebanon, diaspora engagement extends beyond remittances and operates through structured mechanisms, including community hubs, accelerators, digital platforms, and angel networks. These mechanisms connect startups with international investors, mentors, and markets while enhancing visibility and resilience. The chapter also highlights how diaspora business angels reduce financing constraints by mobilizing early-stage capital and signaling credibility to broader investor communities. In addition, knowledge exchange facilitated by diaspora networks supports innovation and strengthens local capabilities. Digital tools further intensify these flows by enabling continuous interaction between global and local actors. Diaspora ecosystems can transform entrepreneurial landscapes by creating sustainable transnational pipelines that support long-term development, institutional resilience, and inclusive growth.

1 Introduction

Diaspora communities play a central role in entrepreneurial ecosystems, particularly in emerging and fragile economies where access to finance, institutional support, and international networks remains limited (Yasin & Hafeez, 2023). Entrepreneurial ecosystems are no longer purely local structures; they increasingly operate through

S. Hajj Safa (✉)
LIRSA Laboratory-Cnam, Paris, France
e-mail: Sanaa.safa@lecnam.net

N. M. Boustani
Saint Joseph University of Beirut, Beirut, Lebanon
e-mail: nada.mallahboustany@usj.edu.lb

H. Mawlawi
East International University, Tripoly, Lebanon
e-mail: hani.mawlawi@eiu.edu.lb

H. Jarrar et al. (eds.), *Diaspora Angel Investing*, Ethnic and Indigenous Business Studies, https://doi.org/10.1007/978-3-032-33088-8_2

multi-scale and transnational connections linking actors, institutions, and resources across borders (Wurth et al., 2022; Yasin & Poulin, 2025). In this context, diaspora actors function as important bridges between home and host countries, acting as "modern middlemen" who facilitate the circulation of knowledge, capital, opportunities, and legitimacy across ecosystems (Terjesen & Elam, 2009). Their transnational embeddedness enables them to transfer not only financial resources, but also expertise, mentorship, credibility, and market access to local entrepreneurial communities (Andrade et al., 2022).

In volatile environments such as Lebanon, characterized by successive crises, institutional fragmentation, economic instability, and limited financing opportunities, diaspora engagement becomes particularly critical. Rather than serving solely as a source of remittances or occasional support, the diaspora can act as an organized transnational engine for entrepreneurial development. Through community hubs, accelerators, digital platforms, angel networks, and investment initiatives, diaspora actors contribute to strengthening startups and SMEs while improving their visibility, resilience, and growth potential.

This chapter looks at how diaspora groups might function in unstable and precarious situations like Lebanon. The chapter examines the circumstances that facilitate or limit the impact of diaspora engagement in multi-crisis situations, drawing on both successful international examples and initiatives that faced institutional obstacles or limitations. In order to improve transnational entrepreneurial pipelines and create long-lasting connections between diaspora networks, innovation, and long-term entrepreneurial development, it concludes by putting forth a number of ecosystem proposals.

2 The Diaspora as a Source of Funding: Transnational Capital, Knowledge, and Legitimacy

2.1 The Diaspora: A Financing Lever

Transnational entrepreneurs help maintain active connections with their countries of origin, facilitating the flow of resources, knowledge and opportunities that diminish structural barriers to entrepreneurship. In developing economies, diaspora actors can play a pivotal role in mobilizing crucial early-stage transnational capital, operating as "diaspora business angels", filling the financing gap, especially for start-ups. They combine financial objectives with emotional attachment, and a commitment to national development allowing them to invest in contexts deemed too risky by traditional investors.

Beyond funding young companies, the diaspora networks share their expertise on market entry, innovative business models and regulatory knowledge while offering access to trusted international ecosystems. Their contributions serve as a signaling effect, boosting startup credibility and attracting further funding. Additionally, they are vital in humanitarian and crisis contexts, where they serve as trusted middlemen that can quickly mobilize resources (Gamlen & Chakma, 2025).

In crisis context like Lebanon, capital from diaspora business angel networks has emerged as an important alternative source of financing, particularly for high-potential sectors, such as fintech, agritech, healthtech, digital services and humanitarian services. Lebanese startups, such as *Toters* (raised $23 million), *Sarwa* (raised $15 million), *Kitopi* (raised more than $800 million) and *Quipup* (raised $45 million), have scaled significantly through funding mobilized by diaspora networks (Keuchkerian, 2025).

2.2 Diaspora and Knowledge Transfer

Knowledge flows and skills development are as critical as financial capital for the sustainability of entrepreneurial ecosystems. In this sense, transnational entrepreneurs who have acquired international knowledge are of great importance in connecting nascent founders in their home countries with key resources such as expertise, talent, transfer of innovation practices and access to financing opportunities. Feldman and Zoller (2016 note that successful and philanthropic entrepreneurs can act as "dealmakers" who play roles that foster connections through which knowledge spreads, thereby reducing the costs associated with engaging in innovative activities and contributing, as a result, to regional dynamism. Both entrepreneurial successes and failures within an ecosystem can generate resources essential to entrepreneurship, such as investment capital, skilled labor, and entrepreneurial know-how (Spigel, 2017).

However, the dissemination of knowledge requires local structured mechanisms such as innovation hubs and accelerators that are capable of structuring interactions and translating global knowledge into locally relevant practices (Goswami & Ivey, 2018). Accelerators in particular act as bridging institutions connecting startups to investors, mentors, and broader ecosystem resources. In Lebanon, local entrepreneurs often face limitations in terms of exposure to international markets and innovation practices. Diaspora actors help bridge this gap by facilitating access to global networks and introducing new approaches related to business growth, governance, and market expansion. Furthermore, the digital revolution has greatly enhanced the capacity of diaspora networks to transmit knowledge. Digital platforms enable real-time interaction among diaspora members and local entrepreneurs, thereby facilitating continuous learning and collaboration. These platforms are instrumental in spreading entrepreneurial knowledge and promoting sustainable competitiveness in emerging economies, as shown by Dabbous et al. (2023).

2.3 The Diaspora: A Vector of Legitimacy

In addition to funding and know-how, diaspora actors are crucial for building legitimacy—an important, but often overlooked, factor in entrepreneurial ecosystems (Yasin et al., 2024). Legitimacy refers to the degree to which entrepreneurial activities are perceived as credible and having the potential to develop the local ecosystem. The literature suggests that legitimacy in transnational contexts is inherently relational and multidimensional, arising at the intersection of organizational, institutional, and geopolitical dynamics. Such a dynamic is shown in empirical studies. For instance, Bolzani et al. (2020) show how transnational entrepreneurs construct organizational legitimacy by blending forms of moral and pragmatic legitimacy from different institutional contexts. Similarly, Williams (2020) shows the efforts of post-conflict states to mobilize diasporas as agents of institutional change, and Liu (2022) demonstrates how diaspora policies can be reoriented to broader geopolitical goals.

In practice, there are three main mechanisms through which diaspora engagement enhances legitimacy. Diaspora investors and mentors first act as quality signals, which reduce uncertainty and enhance the perceived credibility of the startups. Second, diaspora actors contribute to institutional transfers by importing governance standards, norms and practices acquired in their host countries and thus to the institutionalization of entrepreneurial ecosystems (Theodoraki et al., 2022). Third, diaspora networks promote the internationalization of local firms to overcome the "small-size handicap" and the "home-country handicap."

2.4 Toward an Integrated Ecosystem Driven by the Diaspora

As noted by Cantner et al. (2021), entrepreneurial ecosystems evolve through dynamic life cycles, and depend on the effective alignment of actors and resources. But in Lebanon, the diaspora's participation is mostly disjointed and its overall impact is therefore limited. Addressing this challenge requires a more strategic and integrated approach to diaspora engagement that combine capital, knowledge and legitimacy in a coherent framework. This involves building strong intermediary organizations, leveraging digital platforms to foster connectivity, enabling supportive public policies and improving coordination between local and diaspora actors. In this context, diaspora business angels should be viewed, not only as capital providers but as architects of ecosystems capable of structuring sustainable entrepreneurial dynamics and promoting the creation of globally interconnected value chains.

3 The "Local" (Lebanese) Ecosystem- Hubs of Creativity in a Collapsed System

Lebanon's case illustrates the duality of great opportunities and structural constraints. The country's ecosystem is hampered by institutional fragmentation, weak public policy coordination and limited access to financing, despite a globally connected diaspora, strong human capital and emerging support structures. When traditional institutional support systems fail, creativity hubs in a local entrepreneurship ecosystem act as resilient anchors during economic collapse. They connect startups and SMEs to shared resources and diaspora networks, empowering them to sustain their innovative projects.

3.1 Overview of the Lebanese Entrepreneurial Ecosystem

Amid severe economic and political challenges, Lebanon's entrepreneurial ecosystem has proven highly resilient, driven by a dense population of highly skilled, adaptable, and multilingual talent. The ecosystem's initial boom was fueled by *Banque du Liban*'s 2013 Circular 331, which injected up to $400 million into the sector. By 2019, more than 2000 startups were operating in Lebanon, including some notable success stories such as *Diwanee*, *Anghami*, and *Toters* (Euromena Consulting, 2019). Despite the 2019 economic crisis, a dysfunctional banking sector, and 98% Lebanese currency devaluation, Lebanese startups still managed to raise $100–120 million in 2024, primarily achieved through **diaspora networks** (NextStars, 2025).

Lebanon's entrepreneurship ecosystem, ranked #77 worldwide in the 2025 Global Startup Ecosystem Index by *StartupBlink* (2025), functions as an interdependent web of four main pillars supporting the SMEs/startups, as shown in Fig. 1 below.

These four primary pillars—Education, Funding and Finance, Governance, and Business Support— collectively provide the resources, capital, and regulatory framework necessary to support startups and small and medium enterprises (SMEs) in their development. Some of the key business support organizations in Lebanon are highlighted below.

3.2 Community Hubs and co-Working Spaces

In Lebanon, community hubs, co-working spaces and fab labs serve as centralized nodes for knowledge exchange, resource sharing, and professional networking and act as "anchors of resilience" filling the vacuum left by the reduction of traditional public services. Table 1 identifies the main community hubs and co-working spaces that support this anchoring role in Lebanon.

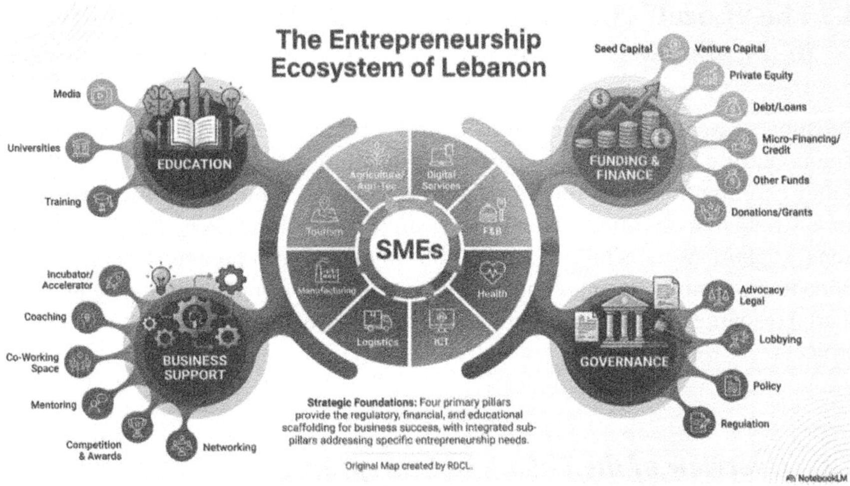

Fig. 1 The Entrepreneurship Ecosystem Map in Lebanon (Simplified from RDCL Report by Naufal (2022))

Table 1 Key Community Hubs/Co-working Spaces in Lebanon

#	Year Founded	Community Hub/ Co-working	Location (s)
1	2002	Berytech	Beirut, mar Roukoz
2	2006	Business incubation Association of Tripoli	Tripoli
4	2012	Beirut Digital District (BDD)	Beirut
5	2016	Antwork	Beirut
6	2021	*HEXA* Lebanon	Choueifat, Beirut
7	2024	*Masahet nour* (space of light)	Tripoli

3.3 Accelerators and Incubators

Given that entrepreneurship is a key driver of economic development and job creation, business accelerators and incubators have become key mechanisms for fostering innovation and supporting startup creation among aspiring student entrepreneurs (Mawlawi, 2025). In Lebanon, amidst the country's economic collapse many accelerator programs have shifted from traditional equity-based models to grant-based or hybrid structures, supported heavily by international agencies, like the EU, UNDP, USAID, and the World Bank. Table 2 maps the leading accelerator programs that structure this support landscape.

To strengthen the global integration of the Lebanese entrepreneurial ecosystem, some local initiatives serve as sites connecting national dynamics to diaspora capital and knowledge transfer. Programs such as *LebHub* exemplify this dynamic by supporting the international expansion of Lebanese startups through mentoring,

Table 2 Leading Accelerator Programs in Lebanon

#	Year Founded	Organization	Main Accelerator Program(s)
1	2002	Berytech	Agrytech, clyntech, ARYAF, LebanonInnovate, WE4f2.0
2	2006	Business incubation Association of Tripoli (BIAT)	SME support program
3	2014	Jadawa06 (formerly Tripoli entrepreneurs Club)	Startup seeds, Mousharakah
4	2016	Neopreneur	Road to entrepreneurship, ladder, Asasat, Tawasol
5	2017	Flat6Labs Beirut	StartMashreq
6	2017	SMART ESA	EdTech accelerator, Boost2idea
7	2019	AUB iPark	Idea validation, Build & Accelerate, go to market, Startup support
8	2025	LebHub	LebHub accelerator

access to investors, and strategic guidance. Similarly, initiatives such as *LebanonInnovate*, implemented by Berytech with the support of the European Union, aim to strengthen the national innovation ecosystem by promoting links between research, industry and entrepreneurship. This program, in addition to its institutional role, indirectly mobilizes diaspora resources by inserting local startups into transnational networks of knowledge, expertise and financing.

3.4 *Financial Support Platforms*

Diaspora support for start-ups takes many forms, from equity investments through business angel networks to participatory finance mechanisms such as crowdfunding. For instance, Beirut Angels brings together local investors and the diaspora to fund early-stage startups. Likewise, projects like *Crowdfarming* Lebanon show the use of crowdfunding as a means to support agricultural projects, and social enterprises such as *FabricAID* leverage hybrid models, with diaspora donations and impact investing.

Mousharakah is a specialized investment matchmaking program designed to bridge the gap between promising startups/SMEs and a network of angel investors that includes diaspora (Jadwa06, 2023). The program was launched in 2022 by Jadwa06 (formerly TEC-Tripoli Entrepreneurs Club), and has provided comprehensive support to help local businesses on refining business models and plans, conducting technical assessments, and on securing funding. So far, the program has successfully supported 12 SMEs and has secured $0.5 million in funding from 15 diaspora angel investors, fostering crucial partnerships and business growth within the entrepreneurial ecosystem in Lebanon (F. Mikati, personal communication, April 27, 2026).

Structured platforms like LIFE, a global network of Lebanese professionals in the diaspora, have proven highly effective in connecting Lebanese founders with global investors through events like "Pitch Nights" in cities such as New York, London, Paris and Dubai. These events connect Lebanese entrepreneurs with global investors and industry leaders. LIFE has supported 56 founders over the past three years, and 13 of their companies have raised over $43 million post participation (Ayoub, 2025).

3.5 Mapping the Local Pipeline: From Idea to Investment-Ready Startups

In Lebanon's fragile market, the entrepreneurial pipeline frequently breaks down in the "valley of death" between the concept phase and early-stage financing due to a severe lack of local liquidity, the evaporation of venture capital, and the burdensome regulatory (El Kadi, 2022). Despite these fractures, the pipeline remains potent due to the enduring strengths of Lebanon's human capital, with continuous support from the ecosystem and Lebanon's diaspora. This is exemplified by many initiatives like Beiurt Angels, *Crowdfarming*, *Mousharakah*, and "Pitch Nights", as discussed in the previous section.

4 Pipeline Innovation in Fragile States: What Works and What Fails?

4.1 Sourcing Challenges Unique to Multi-Crisis Contexts

Overlapping macroeconomic, political and institutional disruptions constrain entrepreneurial pipelines in fragile, multi-crisis environments. In such contexts, currency collapse, regulatory ambiguity, political instability and talent migration weaken how startups are identified, evaluated and financed. These conditions create institutional voids that reduce the volume and quality of investment-ready ventures (Webb et al., 2020).

Currency depreciation and exchange rate volatility complicate valuation by making revenues costs and risks difficult to project. Thus, early-stage investors adopt conservative strategies, including smaller ticket sizes and shorter investment horizons. These dynamics are further exacerbated by political uncertainty which dampens the exit outlook, with investors anticipating few acquisition opportunities and underdeveloped capital markets. In these environments, traditional exit strategies such as IPOs or strategic sales are either delayed or simply not an option.

At the same time, talent flight depletes the pool of skilled human capital in local ecosystems, weakening startup teams and limiting scalability. This is a particularly acute problem in crisis-hit economies, where high-potential entrepreneurs often flee to more stable environments, leaving behind fragmented innovation systems (Yasin, 2022; Yasin et al., 2026). However, legal ambiguity exacerbates these challenges by increasing transaction costs and discouraging formal investment due to uncertainties surrounding contract enforcement and investor protection mechanisms (Khosravi et al., 2023).

In response, investors rely less on formal performance metrics, and more on informal signals, such as founder background, diaspora connections, and network reputation (Skalicka et al., 2022; Topaler & Khan, 2025). Meanwhile, external shocks such as the COVID-19 crisis have revealed the fragility of systems of startup financing with reports of a dramatic contraction of seed-stage investments in times of high volatility (Brown & Rocha, 2020).

4.2 Successful Practices Observed Internationally

Despite these challenges, some fragile and risky ecosystems have shown the ability to support entrepreneurial pipelines by using adaptive strategies and transnational investment models. In Armenia, diaspora investors supported local startups to overcome domestic constraints by providing the capital, mentorship and international networks that have helped them plug into global value chains. Similarly, diaspora engagement has been critical in the fast-growing fintech ecosystem in Nigeria, where cross-border capital flows and digital platforms enable early-stage financing and scaling. In Ukraine, especially in a conflict environment, IT companies supported by the diaspora have demonstrated resilience through the adoption of remote work business models and international clientele, which have insulated them from local market disruptions.

These cases underscore that the success of pipeline development in fragile contexts depends on the integration of local entrepreneurial activity with transnational networks. At the micro level, entrepreneurs employ strategies such as bricolage and resource recombination to deal with institutional constraints (Sydow et al., 2020). At the meso level, intermediaries such as incubators and accelerators mitigate information asymmetry and signal venture quality (Du et al., 2025). At the macro level, diaspora investment provides access to stable financial systems and external markets, thereby offsetting local institutional weaknesses (Gevorkyan, 2021).

4.3 Lessons for Lebanon

The Lebanese case underscores the urgency of rethinking entrepreneurial pipelines to work well in persistent instability. Based on local constraints and international experience, three lessons are drawn for enhancing pipeline resilience and sustainability.

First, de-risking early-stage investment is key. Given the high degree of uncertainty around currency volatility, political instability and weak regulatory frameworks, blended finance mechanisms provide a viable solution. These instruments combine public donor and private capital to mitigate downside risk as well as incentivize investor participation in early-stage ventures (Otunba et al., 2025). Likewise, angel syndication and network-based models of investment are able to share risk among multiple actors and improve deal flow and investment outcomes (Bonini et al., 2018).

Second, trusted cross-border investment frameworks are important to establish. Diaspora investors are a strategic asset for Lebanon, because of their financial capacity, international exposure and integration in global markets. But they need transparent governance structures, predictable legal systems and credible investment channels. In the absence of these conditions, diaspora capital is likely to be diverted toward low risk, non-productive sectors as has been observed in other crisis economies (Siwale, 2018). Policy tools such as diaspora bonds, co-investment platforms and regulatory incentives can improve the alignment of diaspora capital and productive entrepreneurial activity (Gevorkyan, 2021).

Third, community governance should be strengthened. In the absence of strong formal institutions, local ecosystems are increasingly relying on networks of hubs, accelerators and intermediaries to coordinate entrepreneurial activity and to facilitate pipeline development. These actors are responsible for critical functions including venture identification, validation and matching investors while building trust and reducing uncertainty. Therefore, it is crucial to reinforce these community-based structures to ensure the continuity and scalability of startup pipelines in Lebanon.

Figure 2 illustrates the conceptual framework for this chapter to synthesize the interaction between institutional voids, entrepreneurial pipelines and diaspora-enabled de-risking mechanisms in fragile ecosystems.

The above model shows how weak formal institutions—including financial instability, regulatory ambiguity, political uncertainty, and information asymmetry—affect all stages of entrepreneurial development. In response to these constraints, entrepreneurial ecosystems rely on a multi-layered pipeline structure. Community hubs and innovation spaces act as local discovery mechanisms that identify and support entrepreneurial talent. Accelerators and incubators then provide validation, mentorship, and signaling functions that improve venture readiness and reduce information asymmetry. Finally, diaspora investors, angel networks, and digital investment platforms enable cross-border financing and scaling opportunities through transnational capital and knowledge flows. The lower section of the model highlights de-risking mechanisms operating at micro, meso, and macro levels, including

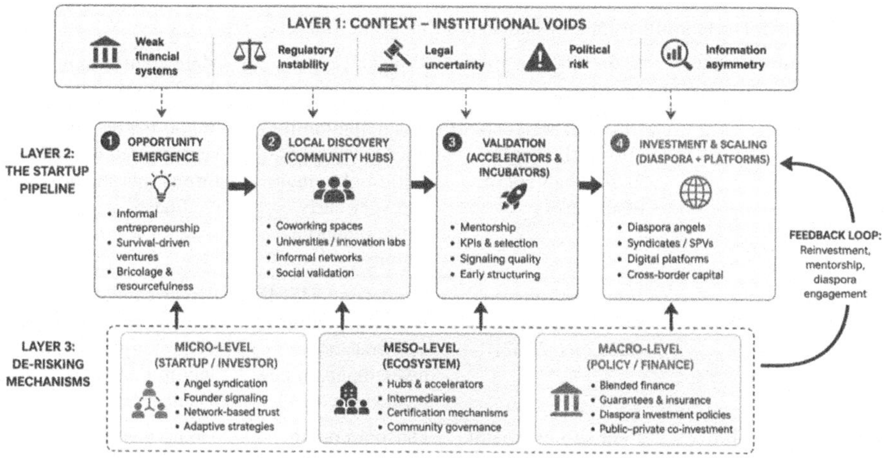

Fig. 2 Startup Pipelines in Fragile Entrepreneurial Ecosystems

syndication, blended finance, governance reforms, and intermediary institutions. The feedback loop emphasizes how successful investments and diaspora engagement can reinforce and sustain the entrepreneurial ecosystem over time.

Diaspora investment in emerging markets operates through several complementary channels rather than one single financing mechanism. Table 3 summarizes how remittances, diaspora direct investment, portfolio instruments, digital platforms, and diaspora angel investors each contribute differently to startup financing and pipeline development. Together, these mechanisms show how diaspora capital can move from informal support for microbusinesses to more structured forms of entrepreneurial finance, combining funding with knowledge, trust, legitimacy, and access to international networks.

Diaspora investment decisions are shaped by mixed motivations and by the specific conditions of the home-country ecosystem. Table 4 summarizes the main drivers, advantages, and constraints that influence whether diaspora capital flows into productive entrepreneurial ventures or shifts toward safer, less innovative sectors.

Diaspora investors also play a specific role within startup ecosystems because they behave partly like business angels while also bringing transnational knowledge, legitimacy, and market access. Table 5 highlights how they contribute to early-stage finance, risk reduction, and ecosystem building.

Table 3 Main Diaspora Investment Channels in Emerging Markets

Diaspora investment channel	Main role in startup financing	Typical use in emerging markets	Main contribution to the pipeline
Remittances	Informal seed capital (Bouzerb et al., 2024; khayreddine et al., 2024)	Financing family microbusinesses, self-employment, and very early entrepreneurial activity	Supports grassroots venture creation before formal investment readiness
Diaspora direct investment (DDI)	Equity or direct investment in firms (Naujoks, 2022)	Supporting MSMEs, informal ventures, and first-mover investments in new businesses	Brings capital, managerial know-how, technology transfer, and international business links
Diaspora portfolio investment	Indirect investment through bonds and capital markets(Bouzerb et al., 2024; khayreddine et al., 2024)	Diaspora bonds, capital market instruments, and state-backed development financing	Strengthens financial systems and channels diaspora capital toward productive sectors
Diasporic crowdlending / digital platforms	Small-scale distributed financing (Mason et al., 2021)	Online loans or platform-based funding for entrepreneurs with limited access to formal credit	Reduces geographic barriers, lowers transaction costs, and connects distant investors to local ventures
Diaspora angels / hybrid investors	Early-stage capital with mentorship and networks (Nyame-Asiamah et al., 2020)	Financing startups while providing advice, legitimacy, and access to foreign markets	Bridges information asymmetry and transforms social trust into investment trust

5 Policy and Ecosystem Recommendations—Building Tomorrow's Transnational Pipeline

The development of a transnational entrepreneurial pipeline requires coordinated action across multiple levels of the ecosystem. Governments and regulators must create credible legal and institutional conditions for diaspora investment, while local accelerators and hubs should structure transparent pipelines that connect promising ventures with diaspora expertise and capital. At the same time, diaspora angel networks need professionalized investment practices, including remote due diligence, syndication, impact measurement, and co-investment mechanisms. Table 6 presents the main recommendations for each stakeholder group.

Table 4 Drivers, Advantages, Constraints of Diaspora Investment Decisions

Dimension	
Main motivations	Diaspora investors combine financial objectives with emotional attachment to the homeland, altruism, social recognition, and the desire to contribute to national development (Spigel & Harrison, 2017, 2018).
Strategic advantages	Their dual embeddedness in home and host countries gives them access to local knowledge, trusted networks, cultural familiarity, and international market connections, reducing information asymmetry compared to external investors (Nyame-Asiamah et al., 2020).
Main barriers	Weak institutions, corruption risks, regulatory complexity, currency volatility, and limited investor protection often discourage diaspora investment in high-growth ventures (Bouzerb et al., 2024; khayreddine et al., 2024)
Risk response	In high-risk environments, diaspora capital may be redirected toward safer sectors such as real estate, consumption activities, or family-based ventures, reducing its potential impact on innovation and startup growth (Grilli, 2018).
Geographic concentration	Concentrated diaspora communities tend to generate stronger entrepreneurial effects because networks are denser, trust is easier to mobilize, and collective investment coordination becomes more feasible (Vaaler, 2013).

Table 5 Diaspora investment contribution to early-stage finance, risk reduction and ecosystem building

Aspect	
Similarity with business angels	Diaspora investors often resemble business angels because they invest at early stages, rely on relational trust, and use informal networks to identify and evaluate opportunities (Alka et al., 2025).
Risk management mechanisms	They reduce risk through co-investment, syndication, informal due diligence, and network-based monitoring, especially where formal financial institutions are weak (Harrison, 2022).
Signaling role	Diaspora equity participation can act as a quality signal, improving startup credibility and facilitating access to international partners, investors, and technology licensing opportunities (Gregorič et al., 2020).
Policy support needed	Their impact increases when governments provide structured investment channels such as diaspora venture funds, bonds, matching schemes, and transparent regulatory frameworks (Naujoks, 2022).
Overall ecosystem contribution	Diaspora investors do more than finance startups; they also provide mentorship, knowledge transfer, market access, and institutional bridging between local ventures and global ecosystems (Ojo et al., 2013).

Table 6 Recommendations for ecosystem stakeholder groups

Stakeholder	Recommendations
Governments and regulators	Develop clear legal frameworks that protect diaspora investors, secure contract enforcement, and reduce political and financial uncertainty. Governments should also simplify administrative procedures, reduce bureaucratic barriers, and introduce tax incentives or preferential treatment for diaspora-backed entrepreneurial investments. Digital identity systems and one-stop investment platforms can improve investor verification, transparency, and trust. Dedicated diaspora agencies can also coordinate communication, provide reliable information, and connect diaspora investors with local entrepreneurial opportunities (Franc et al., 2020; Williams, 2018; Kessy & Shayo, 2022).
Local accelerators and hubs	Build transparent startup funnels that guide ventures from idea generation to investment readiness. This includes clear selection criteria, standardized evaluation tools, progress milestones, and regular reporting mechanisms. Accelerators and hubs should actively integrate diaspora investors through mentorship, demo days, advisory boards, and cross-border investment committees. They should also develop thematic clusters in areas such as AI, healthtech, energy, and fintech to attract specialized diaspora expertise and strengthen sector-based deal flow.
Diaspora angel networks	Adopt structured remote due diligence practices that combine financial analysis, market validation, governance assessment, and founder evaluation. Diaspora angel networks should use syndication models to pool capital, share expertise, reduce individual risk, and increase investment capacity. They should also adopt impact measurement frameworks to assess both financial returns and developmental outcomes. Partnerships with development institutions through blended finance, matching funds, and joint investment vehicles can help scale diaspora investment while reducing exposure to fragile-market risks (Harrison, 2022; Alka et al., 2025).

6 Conclusion

In emerging economies, diaspora investment offers a powerful combination of financial, relational, and strategic resources. Through business angel networks, impact funds, mentoring relationships, and global professional communities, diaspora actors can reduce investment risk, transfer knowledge, open access to international markets, and provide credibility signals that help local startups and SMEs gain legitimacy with investors, institutions, and partners. However, diaspora investing can only succeed where structured pipelines exist to reposition these investors as long-term strategic partners rather than mere donors.

Community hubs, accelerators, and platforms facilitate transparent sourcing, capacity building, and risk-sharing by transforming social trust into financial trust. In this way, diaspora actors serve as pipeline builders, facilitating the movement of capital, expertise, legitimacy, and opportunities across national borders. Finally, while capital can help individual businesses, it is the interconnected and transnational networks that create and sustain robust entrepreneurial ecosystems.

Such pipelines can help Lebanon strategically direct diaspora investment toward high-impact sectors with strong economic, social, and technological potential, such as AI-enabled sourcing and advisory tools, fintech and digital banking, GovTech, healthtech, EdTech, and energy transition. Future pipeline development should increasingly leverage AI sourcing tools, cross-border ESG scoring, and climate-focused deal flow to strengthen the long-term contribution of diaspora networks to innovation and entrepreneurial resilience.

References

Alka, T., Suresh, M., & Raman, R. (2025). Exploring the trajectory of migrant entrepreneurship research: BERTopic modeling. *Journal of Organizational Change Management*. https://doi.org/10.1108/jocm-10-2024-0666

Andrade, R., Pinheiro, P., Carvalho, L., & Rocha, R. (2022). Building a bridge: Knowledge sharing flows into entrepreneurial ecosystems. *Journal of Open Innovation: Technology, Market, and Complexity, 8*(3), 144. https://doi.org/10.3390/joitmc8030144

Bolzani, D., Marabello, S., & Honig, B. (2020). Exploring the multi-level processes of legitimacy in transnational social enterprises. *Journal of Business Venturing*. https://doi.org/10.1016/j.jbusvent.2019.06.002

Bonini, S., Capizzi, V., Valletta, M., & Zocchi, P. (2018). Angel network affiliation and business angels' investment practices. *Journal of Corporate Finance*. https://doi.org/10.1016/j.jcorpfin.2017.12.029

Brown, R., & Rocha, A. (2020). Entrepreneurial uncertainty during the Covid-19 crisis: Mapping the temporal dynamics of entrepreneurial finance. *Journal of Business Venturing Insights, 14*, e00174–e00174. https://doi.org/10.1016/j.jbvi.2020.e00174

Cantner, U., Cunningham, J. A., Lehmann, E. E., & Menter, M. (2021). Entrepreneurial ecosystems: A dynamic lifecycle model. *Small Business Economics, 57*, 407–423. https://doi.org/10.1007/s11187-020-00316-0

Dabbous, A., Aoun Barakat, K., & Kraus, S. (2023). The impact of digitalization on entrepreneurial activity and sustainable competitiveness: A panel data analysis. *Technology in Society, 73, Article 102224*. https://doi.org/10.1016/j.techsoc.2023.102224

Du, J., Li, J., Liang, B., & Yan, Z. (2025). Optimizing sustainable entrepreneurial ecosystems: The role of government-certified incubators in early-stage financing. *Sustainability*. https://doi.org/10.3390/su17093854

Franc, S., Kasel, M., & Kirbiš, I. (2020). Policies for promoting diaspora investment in countries of origin. *Obrazovanje za poduzetništvo, E4E*. https://doi.org/10.38190/ope.10.1.5

Feldman, M. P., & Zoller, T. D. (2016). Dealmakers in place: Social capital connections in regional entrepreneurial economies. In H. Westlund & J. P. Larsson (Eds.), *Handbook of social capital and regional development*. Edward Elgar Publishing EBooks. https://doi.org/10.4337/9781783476831.00011

Gamlen, A., & Chakma, A. (2025). Trusted intermediaries? The role of diasporas in humanitarian assistance. International Journal of Disaster Risk Reduction, *117*, Article 105212. doi:https://doi.org/10.1016/j.ijdrr.2025.105212.

Gevorkyan, A. (2021). Diaspora and economic development: A systemic view. *The European Journal of Development Research, 34*, 1522–1541. https://doi.org/10.1057/s41287-021-00432-x

Goswami, K., & Ivey, R. (2018). Accelerator expertise: Understanding the intermediary role of accelerators in the development of the Bangalore entrepreneurial ecosystem. *Strategic Entrepreneurship Journal, 12*, 117–150. https://doi.org/10.1002/sej.1281

Gregorič, A., Rabbiosi, L., & Santangelo, G. (2020). Diaspora ownership and international technology licensing by emerging market firms. *Journal of International Business Studies, 1-21.* https://doi.org/10.1057/s41267-020-00324-y

Grilli, L. (2018). There must be an angel? Local financial markets, business angels and the financing of innovative start-ups. *Regional Studies, 53*, 620–629. https://doi.org/10.1080/00343404.2018.1479524

Harrison, R. (2022). "Pennies from heaven"? Market failure, circuits of capital and policy support for business angels: The case of cross-border angel investment. *Journal of Business Venturing Insights*. https://doi.org/10.1016/j.jbvi.2022.e00311

Kessy, A., & Shayo, H. (2022). Tanzania's diaspora engagement: The need for a paradigm shift in the diaspora engagement and investment policies. *Research in Globalization*. https://doi.org/10.1016/j.resglo.2022.100095

Khosravi, M., Amiri, M., & Faghih, N. (2023). Ideology and ethics of transitional entrepreneurs: Legitimacy, soft law, and overcoming a distressed economy. *New England Journal of Entrepreneurship*. https://doi.org/10.1108/neje-10-2022-0095

Liu, J. (2022). When diaspora politics meet global ambitions: Diaspora institutions amid China's geopolitical transformations. *International Migration Review, 56*, 1255–1279. https://doi.org/10.1177/01979183211072824

Mason, C., Botelho, T., & Duggett, J. (2021). Promoting cross-border investing by business angels in the European Union. *Regional Studies, 56*, 1391–1403. https://doi.org/10.1080/00343404.2021.1960961

Mawlawi, H. R. (2025). The perceived impact of entrepreneurship education on the journey of student entrepreneurs in Lebanon [thesis, CNAM]. https://theses.fr/s234926.

Naujoks, D. (2022). A transnational research agenda on the determinants, policies, and impacts of diaspora direct investments. *Research in Globalization*. https://doi.org/10.1016/j.resglo.2022.100083

Nyame-Asiamah, F., Amoako, I., Amankwah-Amoah, J., & Debrah, Y. (2020). Diaspora entrepreneurs' push and pull institutional factors for investing in Africa: Insights from African returnees from the United Kingdom. *Technological Forecasting and Social Change, 152*, 119876. https://doi.org/10.1016/j.techfore.2019.119876

Ojo, S., Nwankwo, S., & Gbadamosi, A. (2013). African Diaspora Entrepreneurs. *The International Journal of Entrepreneurship and Innovation, 14*, 289–299. https://doi.org/10.5367/ijei.2013.0126

Otunba, M., Adenuga, A., Sikiru, A., & Gaffar, O. (2025). Designing capital-raising frameworks for agro Enterprises in Underserved and Volatile Economies. *Engineering and Technology Journal*. https://doi.org/10.47191/etj/v10i08.41

Siwale, J. (2018). *Mapping of Diaspora Direct Investment: Critical Areas of Investment., 2018*, 63–85. https://doi.org/10.1007/978-3-319-72047-0_4

Skalicka, M., Zinecker, M., Balcerzak, A., & Pietrzak, M. (2022). Business angels and early stage decision making criteria: Empirical evidence from an emerging market. *Economic Research-Ekonomska Istraživanja, 36*, 25–50. https://doi.org/10.1080/1331677x.2022.2063920

Spigel, B. (2017). The relational Organization of Entrepreneurial Ecosystems. Entrepreneurship Theory and Practice, 41(1), 49–72. https://.doi.org/10.1111/etap.12167.

Sydow, A., Cannatelli, B., Giudici, A., & Molteni, M. (2020). Entrepreneurial workaround practices in severe institutional voids: Evidence from Kenya. *Entrepreneurship Theory and Practice, 46*, 331–367. https://doi.org/10.1177/1042258720929891

Terjesen, S., & Elam, A. (2009). Transnational entrepreneurs venture internationalization strategies: A practice theory approach. *Entrepreneurship Theory and Practice, 33*(5), 1093–1120. https://doi.org/10.1111/j.1540-6520.2009.00336.x

Theodoraki, C., Dana, L.-P., & Caputo, A. (2022). Building sustainable entrepreneurial ecosystems: A holistic approach. *Journal of Business Research, 140*, 346–360. https://doi.org/10.1016/j.jbusres.2021.11.005

Topaler, B., & Khan, H. (2025). Signaling shaped by the context: Early-stage funding in the Turkish startup ecosystem. *Management & Marketing, 20*, 65–77. https://doi.org/10.2478/mmcks-2025-0012

Vaaler, P. (2013). Diaspora concentration and the venture investment impact of remittances. *Journal of International Management, 19*, 26–46. https://doi.org/10.1016/j.intman.2012.11.004

Webb, J., Khoury, T., & Hitt, M. (2020). The influence of formal and informal institutional voids on entrepreneurship. *Entrepreneurship Theory and Practice, 44*, 504–526. https://doi.org/10.1177/1042258719830310

Williams, N. (2018). Mobilising diaspora to promote homeland investment: The progress of policy in post-conflict economies. *Environment and Planning C: Politics and Space, 36*, 1256–1279. https://doi.org/10.1177/2399654417752684

Williams, N. (2020). Moving beyond financial remittances: The evolution of diaspora policy in post-conflict economies. *International Small Business Journal: Researching Entrepreneurship, 38*, 41–62. https://doi.org/10.1177/0266242619878064

Wurth, B., Stam, E., & Spigel, B. (2022). Toward an entrepreneurial ecosystem research program. *Entrepreneurship Theory and Practice, 46*(3), 729–778. https://doi.org/10.1177/1042258721998948

Yasin, N. (2022). Cold grass or Hot Sands: A comparative study of immigrant Punjabi-Pakistani entrepreneurs in London and Dubai. *Strategic Change: Briefings in Entrepreneurial Finance., 31*(4), 1–10.

Yasin, N., & Hafeez, K. (2023). Three waves of immigrant entrepreneurship. *A Cross-National Comparative Study, Small Business Economics: An Entrepreneurship Journal., 60*(1), 1281–1306. https://doi.org/10.1007/s11187-022-0065z

Yasin, N., Hafeez, K., Haq, M., Haq, F., & Zahoor, & N, Noaman, S. (2026). Take a break: A typology of immigrant Enterprise growth strategies in non-traditional entrepreneurship settings. *Journal of Entrepreneurship in Emerging Economies*. https://doi.org/10.1108/JEEE-09-2025-0568

Yasin, N., & Poulin, M. (2025). Developing a nation of entrepreneurs: The integral role of immigrant entrepreneurship for The United Arab Emirates vision 2030. In C. Margaça, A. Walmsley, & H. Knörr (Eds.), *Immigrant entrepreneurship, religion, and ethnicity: Cases from Europe, Africa, and Asia* (pp. 187–204). Routledge. https://doi.org/10.4324/9781003489214-12

Yasin, N., Hafeez, K., & Salamzadeh, A. (2024). A cross-country comparative ethnographic analysis of immigrant enclave entrepreneurship. *Qualitative Market Research: An International Journal, 28*(1), 1–37. https://doi.org/10.1108/QMR-11-2023-0164

Websites

Ayoub, K. (2025, May 29). Lebanese Startups Tackle Real-World Challenges with LIFE's Global Support.. https://executive-bulletin.com/ngo/lebanese-startups-tackle-real-world-challenges-with-lifes-global-support.

El Kadi, S. (2022). Lebanon's startup ecosystem is struggling. In *Can the trend be reversed? Fast company Middle East|the future of tech*. Innovation. https://fastcompanyme.com/impact/lebanons-startup-ecosystem-is-struggling-can-the-trend-be-reversed/

Euromena Consulting. (2019). The entrepreneurship ecosystem in Lebanon: Rise and road ahead. https://euromenaconsulting.com/insight-details-225.

Jadwa06. (2023). Jadwa06 Website-Mousharakah. https://jadwa06.com/our-services/mousharakah/

Keuchkerian, K. (2025, July). *These 5 Lebanese-Led Startups Are Among The 50 Most-Funded In The Middle East*. https://the961.com/top-funded-lebanese-led-startups-mena-forbes/

Khayreddine, B., Khoualed, A., & Makhloufi, A. (2024). Diaspora investments as a mechanism for financing developing economies: A review of the Nigerian diaspora bond experience. *Journal*

of Public Administration, Finance and Law, 32, 149–164. https://doi.org/10.47743/jopafl-2024-32-11
Naufal, N. (2022). RDCL Report: SME Innovation & Growth Support. RDCL. https://rdcl.org.lb/wp-content/uploads/2022/06/RDCL-SME-ecosystem_Innovation-Growth.pdf
NextStars. (2025, November 6). Lebanon: Innovation Against All Odds. NextStars. https://nextstars.ca/2025/11/06/lebanon-innovation-against-all-odds/
Spigel, B., & Harrison, R. T. (2018). Toward a process theory of entrepreneurial ecosystems. *Strategic Entrepreneurship Journal, 12*(1), 151–168. https://doi.org/10.1002/sej.1268
StartupBrink. (2025). Lebanon Startup Ecosystem—Rankings, Startups, and Insights. The Startup Ecosystem of Lebanon. https://www.startupblink.com/startup-ecosystem/lebanon

Trust Proxies and Due Diligence across Borders: How Diaspora Angels Turn Familiarity into Verifiable Evidence

Gozde Inal Cavlan, Constance Van Horne, Marc Audi, Tehreem Fatima, Ali Tariq, and Razan Al-Masri

Abstract This chapter examines how trust is built, tested, and institutionalized in cross-border diaspora angel investing. The central claim is deliberately cautious. Familiarity can improve access and reduce search costs, but it does not remove the need for due diligence. Mature investing depends on the ability to convert relational confidence into evidence that can survive external scrutiny. Synthesizing research on entrepreneurial signaling, investor learning, cross-border venture finance, and diaspora entrepreneurship, the chapter distinguishes between useful trust proxies and dangerous shortcuts. It then outlines a layered due diligence architecture suited to thin markets and geographically distant deals, where documentary quality, founder reputation, and institutional reliability vary widely. The final section shows how the deal structure continues due diligence after closing through syndication, milestone design, information rights, and monitoring arrangements. The result is a practical framework for conducting disciplined diaspora angel investing across borders without confusing social proximity with investment certainty.

G. Inal Cavlan (✉)
Department of Business Administration, Altinbas Cyprus University, Nicosia-Cyprus, Turkey
e-mail: gozde.inal@wpu.edu.tr

C. Van Horne · M. Audi · R. Al-Masri
Entrepreneurship and Innovation Centre, Abu Dhabi School of Management, Abu Dhabi, United Arab Emirates
e-mail: c.v.horne@adsm.ac.ae

M. Audi
e-mail: m.aoudi@adsm.ac.ae

R. Al-Masri
e-mail: r.masri@adsm.ac.ae

T. Fatima
University of Sargodha, Sargodha, Pakistan

A. Tariq
Management Science, Unviersity of Lahore, Sargodha, Pakistan
e-mail: ali.tariq@lbs.uol.edu.pk

H. Jarrar et al. (eds.), *Diaspora Angel Investing*, Ethnic and Indigenous Business Studies, https://doi.org/10.1007/978-3-032-33088-8_3

1 Introduction

Cross-border angel investing rarely fails because founders and investors do not speak to one another. It fails because they speak from different evidence environments. Founders know the local context, the informal reputation system, and the practical barriers they have already overcome. Investors, by contrast, need signals that can survive distance, later scrutiny, and legal accountability. Diaspora ties can narrow that gap, but they do not erase it. The real challenge is to turn familiarity into evidence that other serious actors would also accept (Riddle et al., 2010; Hain et al., 2016; Mason et al., 2022).

That problem is acute in early-stage finance because uncertainty is already high before geography enters the picture. Product risk, founder risk, execution risk, and financing risk are all present. Once a deal becomes cross-border, additional questions arise. Can the investor verify the founder's claims without relying only on community reputation? Can customer traction be checked independently? Are legal records, beneficial ownership details, and corporate authorizations clear enough for a foreign shareholder to rely on? Mature due diligence begins by taking those questions seriously rather than assuming that trust alone can carry them.

The literature offers a useful distinction here. Relational trust can open the door, but institutional trust determines how far the deal can go. A trusted introduction may justify a first meeting or a first customer call. It cannot justify skipping verification of the cap table, the legal entity, the revenue quality, or the permissions needed to move money and enforce rights. Cross-border investing becomes durable only when social trust and institutional verification reinforce one another rather than substitute for one another (Li & Zahra, 2012; Hain et al., 2016).

This chapter, therefore, treats trust as a discipline rather than a feeling. It explains why trust is the central challenge in diaspora angel deals, identifies the proxies most useful across borders, develops a layered due diligence approach, and shows how the investment instrument itself can continue the verification process after the initial closing.

Cross-border early-stage investing makes this issue a first-order problem because evidence is never evenly distributed. Founders know the business more intimately than investors do; local communities know the founders better than foreign investors do; and the documents available at the seed stage rarely settle the matter on their own. The result is that investors rely on trust proxies long before they can rely on full verification. A mature understanding of these proxies is therefore essential. They are not shortcuts to avoid diligence. They are the signs that tell investors where diligence is worth the cost (Mason & Stark, 2004; Colombo, 2021; Mestwerdt et al., 2025).

Diaspora angels operate in the sharpest version of this problem because they are close enough to receive warm introductions and far enough to face real enforcement, compliance, and monitoring constraints. That combination makes them unusually good at noticing qualitative signals, but also unusually vulnerable to overreading them. A founder may be genuinely respected in the community yet unready for investor-grade reporting, legal hygiene, or cross-border execution. The literature on

Table 1 A practical due diligence matrix for cross-border diaspora angel deals

Risk area	Useful trust proxy	Preferred verification method	Likely deal response
Founder quality	Relevant operating record and strong independent references	Reference calls, employment history checks, and founder consistency across meetings	Proceed only if execution credibility is supported by evidence
Commercial demand	Named customers, paid pilots, repeat use, clear problem ownership	Customer calls, invoices, contracts, retention, or reorder evidence	Tie investment size or tranches to validated demand
Financial credibility	Coherent unit economics and transparent use of funds	Bank records, management accounts, cash runway, and budget review	Reduce ticket size where evidence is partial but promising
Legal cleanliness	Clear incorporation, cap table, and ownership of key assets	Corporate filings, shareholder documents, IP assignment review, and local counsel check	Do not close until control rights and ownership are documented
Cross-border readiness	Ability to report, communicate, and comply across jurisdictions	Data room quality, reporting cadence tests, and compliance checklist	Add reporting obligations and staged governance support
Syndicate reliability	Committed local and external co-investors with relevant expertise	Lead investor diligence note, role clarity, co-investor calls	Use syndication to distribute verification work and post-investment monitoring
Regulatory exposure	An experienced local operator or counsel can explain the licensing and permitting landscape.	Licensing memo, permit copies, regulatory status check	Proceed only when non-compliance risk is bounded and remediation is realistic
Capital movement and ownership	Transparent banking route and clearly identified beneficial owners	KYC pack, sanctions screening, shareholder register, bank confirmation, where feasible	Pause the deal if funds cannot move cleanly or ownership cannot be established confidently

(continued)

Table 1 (continued)

Risk area	Useful trust proxy	Preferred verification method	Likely deal response
Intellectual property and data rights	The founder's explanation aligns with the contracts and product architecture.	Assignment agreements, code repository review, vendor and employment contracts, and data processing terms	Condition closing on the cleanup of ownership gaps and data rights uncertainty
Post-investment reporting readiness	The founder shows willingness to report clearly and on schedule	Sample reporting pack, KPI definitions, reserved matters list	Use tranching and information rights if reporting maturity is still developing

Source: Author's own elaboration based on Mason and Stark (2004), Hain et al. (2016), Colombo (2021), Bonini et al. (2018), Mason et al. (2022), and Mestwerdt et al. (2025)

internationalized angel investing repeatedly shows that the gain from familiarity is highest when it is paired with explicit verification routines rather than private confidence alone (Riddle et al., 2010; Hain et al., 2016; Croce et al., 2023).

Diaspora angel investing sits within a wider immigrant entrepreneurship problem in which familiarity, ethnicity, and shared background can open access to opportunity while also creating dependence on bounded networks, informal legitimacy, and uneven resource mobilization. Comparative studies of immigrant entrepreneurs show that co-ethnic and diaspora ties often support venture creation, market entry, and early-stage trust formation, but they may also reproduce over-embeddedness, financial exclusion, and unequal access to institutional forms of capital (Yasin, 2022; Yasin & Hafeez, 2023; Yasin et al., 2024a, 2024b; Yasin et al., 2025a; Yasin et al., 2025b). This is particularly important in cross-border investment settings because the same relational infrastructures that reduce search costs may also create false confidence when trust is not translated into documentary, commercial, and legal evidence. Recent work on immigrant entrepreneurship and multi-capital mobilization further suggests that sustainable entrepreneurial growth depends on the conversion of social, ethnic, experiential, and financial resources into institutionally legible forms of legitimacy that can travel beyond the original community setting (Yasin & Poulin, 2025; Yasin et al., 2026a; Yasin et al., 2026b). The key issue for diaspora angels is therefore not whether diaspora ties are useful, but whether they can be converted into portable forms of verification that withstand scrutiny from co-investors, legal advisers, later-stage financiers, and other actors outside the original trust network.

2 Why Trust Is the Core Problem in Cross-Border Angel Deals

Entrepreneurial readiness in diaspora investment settings also depends on the wider institutional and educational ecosystems through which founders learn to present, evidence, and professionalize their ventures. Research on entrepreneurship education, incubation, university-industry collaboration, and enterprise learning in the UAE and wider MENA region shows that entrepreneurial capability is not produced by motivation alone, but through structured exposure to markets, mentors, simulations, institutional resources, and practice-based learning environments (Yasin & Khansari, 2021a, 2021b; Yasin & Gilani, 2022; Yasin & Gilani, 2022a; Yasin et al., 2022, 2023a, 2023b; Yasin & Nabi, 2026a, 2026b). This matters for diaspora angels because many early-stage ventures may be commercially promising but institutionally under-prepared, lacking investor-grade reporting, formal governance routines, financial documentation, or the ability to translate local traction into externally verifiable evidence.

Case-based and practice-oriented work on entrepreneurial learning, technology adoption, incubation, and enterprise development further suggests that founders often require intermediary support to move from informal opportunity recognition toward scalable, financeable, and institutionally credible growth pathways (Yasin, 2013; Yasin et al., 2022; Hyams-Ssekasi and Yasin, 2022; Yasin and Khansari, 2022; Yasin et al., 2024). For diaspora investors, due diligence should therefore be understood not only as a screening mechanism, but also as a developmental process through which weakly formalized ventures are assessed, disciplined, and prepared for more demanding forms of capital.

Distance increases uncertainty in at least three ways. First, it weakens informal observation. Investors cannot easily visit customers, inspect facilities, or assess how a founder behaves in routine operating contexts. Second, it raises the cost of correction. If an early impression proves wrong, the investor is farther from the problem and slower to intervene. Third, it amplifies institutional variation. Even basic issues such as share registration, tax treatment, anti-money laundering checks, and enforcement can differ sharply across jurisdictions. That is why trust is not a soft topic in cross-border finance. It is part of the transaction architecture (Li & Zahra, 2012; Hain et al., 2016).

Diaspora investors can reduce some of this friction because they often understand how reputations circulate within a corridor. They may know which founder profiles have genuine standing and which local endorsements are merely ceremonial. However, that familiarity can create a dangerous illusion. The fact that an investor can better understand the context does not mean the context itself is reliable enough for investment. Institutional weakness remains institutional weakness, even when the investor understands it intimately (Riddle et al., 2010; Park & Tuxhorn, 2025).

Cross-border evidence on venture and angel investing reinforces this point. Relational and institutional trust both matter for whether investors enter a deal, but they do different jobs. Relational trust lowers the threshold for engagement. Institutional trust affects whether investors can scale their commitment and defend their rights. In other words, a deal can start with the first form, but it cannot mature without the second (Hain et al., 2016; Jääskeläinen & Maula, 2014).

This is why diaspora angels should be cautious about the language of intuitive conviction. Many investors develop pattern recognition, and investor experience clearly matters. At the same time, experienced angels learn not to romanticize their own confidence. The more seasoned they become, the more likely they are to separate a promising narrative from a verified investment case. Experience sharpens judgment by improving the quality of questions, not by making evidence unnecessary (Botelho et al., 2023; Croce et al., 2023).

The practical implication is simple. In diaspora investing, trust should determine where diligence starts, not where it stops. That sounds modest, but it is one of the most important disciplines in the field.

The first discipline, then, is to rank trust proxies by the kind of claim they actually support. A respected family name or community endorsement may signal basic legitimacy and social accountability, but it says little about product-market fit. An investor who confuses those categories tends to under-diligence the venture's commercial core. By contrast, founder consistency across meetings, customer reference quality, or clear evidence of prior execution usually supports much stronger inferences about operability. Good investors, therefore, treat proxies as claim-specific. They ask what exactly this signal makes more believable and what it leaves unresolved.

This distinction becomes more valuable across borders because some proxies decay as soon as the deal leaves the original social setting. A recommendation that carries enormous weight in one city may mean very little to a co-investor abroad. The same is true of many local awards, media profiles, or ecosystem endorsements. What matters is whether the signal can travel. Signals tied to paid customers, repeat usage, prior venture exits, sector reputation, or strong third-party diligence are far more portable than those tied mainly to communal familiarity. That is one of the clearest lessons from work on signaling, cross-border venture investing, and diaspora entrepreneurship (Riddle et al., 2010; Hain et al., 2016; Colombo, 2021).

A practical implication follows. Cross-border investors should document which proxies they currently rely on and why. Doing so forces a distinction between what is known, what is inferred, and what remains to be checked. That small discipline often prevents the most common failure in diaspora deals: a socially convincing narrative silently hardens into an investment thesis before the investor has gathered commercial proof.

3 Which Trust Proxies Travel Well, and which Ones Do Not

Early-stage investing always relies on signals. The question is which signals travel across borders without losing meaning. Research on entrepreneurial financing shows that signals are useful when they reduce information asymmetry in ways that third parties can also interpret. In cross-border settings, the most durable signals are usually those that can be independently inspected, such as recurring revenue, signed contracts, customer retention, audited or at least well-organized accounts, regulatory permissions, and a legally clean corporate structure (Colombo, 2021).

Founder biography matters too, but only when it points to execution rather than aura. Prior start-up experience, relevant technical expertise, credible industry references, and evidence of building teams or selling to demanding customers are much stronger trust proxies than public visibility or broad community admiration. Mason and Stark's classic work on what investors look for remains useful here because it reminds us that commercial competence and management quality outrank presentation style once the investment decision becomes serious (Mason & Stark, 2004; Colombo, 2021).

Relational signals still have value. A recommendation from a known operator, a co-investor with local credibility, or a respected diaspora intermediary can help investors focus scarce diligence resources. More recent research on cross-border signaling in South African and European angel deals shows precisely how entrepreneurs and investors rely on multiple signal layers when local and foreign evaluative standards do not perfectly overlap. The point is not to reject soft signals. It is to use them as routing devices rather than as proof in themselves (Mestwerdt et al., 2025).

Some signals, by contrast, do not travel well. Generic media attention, local political proximity, informal employment claims, and verbal statements about customer enthusiasm may impress insiders while carrying little weight abroad. Community reputation can also be misleading when it reflects family standing rather than venture capability. The danger is not merely being fooled. It is building a financing story that later investors will refuse because the original screening process generated little transferable evidence (Riddle et al., 2010; Park & Tuxhorn, 2025).

There is a second danger here that receives less attention. Investors can become so wary of soft signals that they create false negatives, dismissing founders who lack polish but possess real commercial traction. This is particularly common in emerging or under-networked ecosystems where documentation quality may lag behind business quality. The answer is not to lower standards. It is to distinguish between evidence that is missing because the business is weak and evidence that is missing because the venture has not yet been coached into an investor-ready presentation. Diaspora angels often add value precisely when they can tell those two conditions apart and then help a strong but underprepared founder close the gap.

A helpful practical distinction is to classify proxies into hard, relational, and institutional categories. Hard proxies concern measurable performance. Relational proxies concern who is willing to stake their reputation on the founder. Institutional proxies concern whether the company exists in a governance and legal form that can be relied upon. Strong cross-border diligence requires some combination of all three. When one category is missing, the deal is usually fragile, even if the other two look promising (Hain et al., 2016; Colombo, 2021).

A second discipline is to ask whether the proxy improves the odds of truth-telling or merely the investor's comfort. These are not the same thing. Warm introductions and shared background often lower perceived social risk, but commercial risk remains. Experienced angels, therefore, look for signals that create accountability outside the relationship itself. Customer references, qualified local counsel, known co-investors, audited transaction histories where feasible, and evidence of prior operator performance all matter because they can be checked by someone who is not emotionally invested in the founder's story (Mason & Stark, 2004; Edelman et al., 2017; Botelho et al., 2023).

It also helps to differentiate between hard, relational, and institutional trust. Hard trust comes from metrics, contracts, and documented performance. Relational trust comes from people willing to put their own reputation behind the founder. Institutional trust comes from incorporation quality, banking traceability, legal enforceability, and regulatory compliance. Cross-border diligence rarely succeeds with only one of these. A socially compelling founder with weak institutional foundations is still risky. A formally compliant company with no reliable commercial evidence is equally fragile. The strongest diaspora deals show enough in all three categories to survive scrutiny by outsiders.

Investor experience changes how these signals are handled. Less experienced angels often overvalue founder charisma or proximity because those cues are vivid and easy to process. More experienced angels tend to break down the opportunity, compare the story to other deals they have seen, and ask where the next investor will be skeptical. Research on business angel learning and syndication suggests that this move from impressionistic confidence to explicit pattern recognition is one of the main ways investment quality improves over time (Paul & Whittam, 2010; Bonini et al., 2018; Botelho et al., 2023). Table 1 translates this discipline into a practical due diligence matrix for cross-border diaspora angel deals.

In practice, a minimum evidence pack can dramatically improve decision quality. Even for small rounds, investors should expect a basic incorporation file, cap table, beneficial ownership disclosure, founder resumes, core customer or pilot evidence, key contracts where available, and a simple explanation of how funds will be used over the next milestone period. Requiring that pack does more than support the current decision. It trains the venture to maintain records in the format that future investors, acquirers, and lenders are likely to request.

Another implication is that proxy weights should vary by sector. In regulated activities such as health, finance, agritech inputs, or cross-border payments, institutional proof has to carry more weight because regulatory failure can destroy the venture regardless of founder credibility. In software or business services, customer proof and product adoption may matter earlier. Good diaspora investors do not mechanically apply a universal checklist. They adjust the diligence emphasis based on the business's real failure modes.

A second implication concerns geography. When the home market is institutionally weaker or documentation practices are inconsistent, investors should not react by demanding impossible perfection from founders. They should react by becoming more explicit about thresholds, contingencies, and remediation steps. That approach keeps diligence realistic without becoming indulgent. It recognizes that the goal is not to punish young firms for operating in difficult contexts, but to know exactly what must be cleaned up before more capital can arrive.

4 A Layered Due Diligence Architecture for Diaspora Angel Deals

Sound cross-border due diligence usually starts with a rapid screening layer rather than a full legal process. At this stage, the investor checks whether the opportunity is real enough to merit deeper work. Typical questions include whether the company is properly incorporated, whether the founder's story is consistent across documents and conversations, whether there is evidence of paying customers or a credible pilot path, and whether there are obvious compliance or sanctions risks. This first pass does not produce certainty, but it prevents wasted effort on non-investable opportunities.

Once a deal clears that threshold, commercial diligence should come next. The aim is not to demand institutional quality reporting from a very young firm. The aim is to verify the commercial claims that justify the investment logic. Customer reference calls, cohort retention where relevant, channel partner validation, proof of payment, and a sober reading of margin structure are usually more revealing than a polished pitch deck. Angels who operate through networks or groups often improve decision quality precisely because they can divide this work across members with sector knowledge (Paul & Whittam, 2010; Bonini et al., 2018).

Financial and legal diligence then need to translate the business into something enforceable. This includes checking the cap table, prior shareholder promises, employee equity arrangements, intellectual property ownership, board authorization, and any restrictions on foreign investment or capital movement. In a diaspora context, beneficial ownership and source-of-funds checks matter as well, not because the founders are suspect, but because later institutional investors will expect clean records from the beginning. Weak paper trails are much easier to prevent early than to repair later (Jääskeläinen & Maula, 2014; Mason et al., 2022).

The diligence process should also test cross-border execution capacity. A founder may be excellent locally but unprepared for the documentation rhythm, reporting discipline, and stakeholder management that international investors expect. That gap is not fatal. In fact, it is common. The issue is whether the founder can learn and whether the investor is willing to support that learning without excusing chronic opacity. Studies of investor experience suggest that better angels become more explicit about these capabilities over time because they know how quickly operational confusion can become governance risk (Botelho et al., 2023; Croce et al., 2023).

Finally, due diligence should produce a deal memo that distinguishes verified facts from assumptions and unresolved questions. That discipline is valuable because memory tends to sanitize uncertainty once enthusiasm grows. A clear record of what was checked, what remains contingent, and which risks are being deliberately accepted helps both the investor and any future syndicate partner. In cross-border investing, clear documentation is not bureaucracy. It is part of the risk control system.

Commercial diligence deserves particular emphasis because it is often where relationship-led deals are weakest. In many cross-border settings, founders can tell a persuasive growth story long before there is enough evidence to support the implied valuation. The task is not to demand large company reporting from a start-up. It is to verify the narrow claims that make the investment case credible. Who exactly is buying, how often, at what gross margin, under what switching costs, and with what sales cycle? Answers to those questions travel much better than narrative enthusiasm. Work on investor criteria and cross-border angel activity suggests that disciplined attention to these operational details is what separates scalable confidence from polite optimism (Mason & Stark, 2004; Mason et al., 2022; Mestwerdt et al., 2025).

Legal diligence also needs a diaspora-specific lens. Investors should not assume that because a founder is known socially, the company's legal architecture is clean. Missing board approvals, undocumented shareholder promises, informal nominee arrangements, or intellectual property owned personally rather than by the company can all undermine later financings. The same is true of beneficial ownership opacity, politically exposed persons risk, sanctions exposure, or sector licenses that do not extend to the activity described in the pitch. These are not edge cases. They are predictable points of fragility in young firms operating across multiple jurisdictions.

Site visits and local partners remain powerful when the deal size justifies them, but they should be used selectively. The goal is not to recreate institutional private equity diligence for a seed round. The goal is to verify the few issues that, if wrong, would fundamentally change the decision. A short customer visit, a warehouse check, or a joint meeting with local counsel may reveal more than weeks of desk research. Good investors focus on decisive uncertainty, not exhaustive paperwork.

A further discipline is to decide explicitly when to stop. Not every unresolved issue deserves endless investigation. Some are deal-breaking, some are priceable, and some can be monitored post-closing. Cross-border angels improve when they classify issues in those terms instead of treating diligence as a binary choice between comfort and rejection. A questionable founder reference may be fatal. A messy but remediable data room may justify a smaller first check with tighter reporting. A customer concentration issue may require tranching rather than abandonment. The quality of the investment process often depends less on finding certainty than on assigning the right response to each uncertainty.

5 Deal Structure as the Continuation of Due Diligence

A sophisticated diaspora angel does not treat diligence as something that ends at signing. Good deal design carries verification forward. Milestone-based tranching is one example. When part of the round is released only after specific commercial or regulatory achievements are documented, the investor gains additional evidence without forcing the founder into endless proof rituals. Tranching works best when milestones are objective, material, and tied to the real bottlenecks of the business rather than to cosmetic targets.

Syndication plays a similar role. Cross-border deals benefit when at least one investor has local operating knowledge, and another has external market or follow-on finance credibility. Research on angel network affiliation and internationalized angel groups shows that syndicates can improve screening, diversify judgment, and strengthen post-investment support, provided the members are genuinely engaged rather than passively attached to the round (Paul & Whittam, 2010; Bonini et al., 2018; Wesemann & Antretter, 2023).

Information rights are another continuation of diligence. Monthly or quarterly reporting, budget discipline, notice around major contracts, and reserved matters for exceptional decisions do more than protect investors. They also keep the company financially sound. Many future diligence problems are simply the accumulated result of not asking for clean information early enough. For diaspora deals, this is especially important because later investors will not have access to the relationship history that enabled the first check.

Post-investment monitoring should remain proportionate. The goal is not to smother the founder or to treat every variance as a governance failure. The goal is to maintain a credible chain of evidence between the original investment thesis and the company's evolving reality. Investors who do this well preserve trust precisely because they make expectations explicit. They show that confidence and accountability can coexist, which often distinguishes a one-off diaspora check from a repeatable cross-border investment practice (Jääskeläinen & Maula, 2014; Mason et al., 2022).

In that sense, the best trust proxy is not a personal bond at all. It is a process that turns uncertain relationships into increasingly verifiable performance. That is what makes a diaspora angel deal attractive to the next layer of capital rather than remaining permanently dependent on the original circle of familiarity.

Syndication reinforces this logic because it allows different investors to validate different parts of the case. A locally embedded angel may know whether the founder can execute in the home market, while a sector specialist abroad may be better placed to assess technical defensibility or customer expansion. A disciplined syndicate documents those differences instead of blending them into a vague collective confidence. That division of diligence work is especially valuable in diaspora deals because no single investor usually sees the whole picture at once.

The post-signing phase is especially important in diaspora investing because the original trust proxies weaken unless a reliable reporting rhythm replaces them. Monthly updates, covenant compliance, notice around key hires and contracts, and transparent use of proceeds all make the company more inspectable. This is not a bureaucratic preference. It is how the investor preserves the right to rely less on private familiarity over time. A venture that reports well becomes easier to support, syndicate, and defend in front of later investors.

Reserved matters and milestone-based tranching also matter because they translate diligence findings into control points that founders can understand. When the investor knows that customer concentration, licensing, or unit economics remain unresolved, the deal should reflect this by including objective, commercially meaningful conditions. Vague concern is a poor governance tool. Specific follow-on conditions are much more effective because they align expectations without pretending that uncertainty has disappeared.

There is, finally, an ethical dimension. Diaspora investors often enjoy social authority in founder communities. Used well, that authority can professionalize the deal and protect both sides from ambiguity. Used badly, it can blur the line between mentorship and coercion or between family deference and consent. A mature due diligence culture, therefore, protects founders as well as investors. It makes the basis of trust explicit, documents obligations clearly, and reduces the risk that later disappointment will be rewritten as betrayal.

This is one reason disciplined investors often preserve relationships even when they decline the deal. A careful no, backed by specific reasons and a clear remediation path, protects both the founder's dignity and the investor's credibility. In corridor-based ecosystems where actors meet again, that matters. It also improves the market because founders learn what future capital will demand. Trust, in that sense, is not only about who gets funded. It is also about whether the process leaves the ecosystem more professional after a negative decision.

6 Conclusion

Trust matters in diaspora angel investing because cross-border deals are built on incomplete evidence. However, the mature lesson from the literature is that trust is most useful when it sharpens diligence rather than replacing it. Social proximity can reveal opportunities, guide attention, and accelerate first contact. It cannot, by itself, validate revenue, legal clarity, governance quality, or cross-border execution capacity.

The strongest diaspora angels, therefore, behave less like patrons and more like disciplined translators. They preserve the advantages of corridor familiarity while insisting on evidence that can travel beyond the original relationship network. When that discipline is carried from screening into deal structure and post-investment monitoring, trust becomes an asset that compounds over time. Without it, familiarity remains local and fragile. With it, diaspora capital becomes investable to others as well.

The best cross-border angels do not eliminate uncertainty. They organize it. They know which signals are worth following, which claims require hard proof, and which weaknesses can be managed through structure rather than optimism. That is what turns diaspora familiarity from a fragile private advantage into a disciplined investment practice that later capital can take seriously.

For founders, this means that a sophisticated investor is not signaling distrust by asking for clear evidence. Quite the opposite. The request for structured diligence is often the clearest sign that the investor is trying to build a company that can survive beyond the original relationship network. Ventures that embrace that discipline early often discover that better records, clearer reporting, and cleaner legal architecture also improve internal decision-making, not just investor confidence.

For investors, the lasting advantage of diaspora familiarity is therefore not that it replaces formal process, but that it helps formal process begin in the right place.

It directs attention toward the opportunities worth testing and the claims worth verifying. Once that discipline is established, trust becomes cumulative rather than fragile. Each round of evidence makes it easier to believe, easier to monitor, and easier to finance again.

References

Bonini, S., Capizzi, V., Valletta, M., & Zocchi, P. (2018). Angel network affiliation and business angels' investment practices. *Journal of Corporate Finance, 50*, 592–608. https://doi.org/10.1016/j.jcorpfin.2017.12.029

Botelho, T., Harrison, R., & Mason, C. (2023). Business angel investment as an informal learning process: Does experience matter? *British Journal of Management, 34*(1), 321–342. https://doi.org/10.1111/1467-8551.12583

Colombo, O. (2021). The use of signals in new venture financing: A review and research agenda. *Journal of Management, 47*(1), 237–259. https://doi.org/10.1177/0149206320911090

Croce, A., Schwienbacher, A., & Ughetto, E. (2023). Internationalization of business angel investments: The role of investor experience. *International Business Review, 32*, 102033. https://doi.org/10.1016/j.ibusrev.2022.102033

Edelman, L. F., Manolova, T. S., & Brush, C. G. (2017). Angel investing: A literature review. *Foundations and Trends in Entrepreneurship, 13*(4–5), 265–439. https://doi.org/10.1561/0300000051

Hain, D., Johan, S., & Wang, D. (2016). Determinants of cross-border venture capital investments in emerging and developed economies: The effects of relational and institutional trust. *Journal of Business Ethics, 138*(4), 743–764. https://doi.org/10.1007/s10551-015-2772-4

Hyams-Sesseki, D., & Yasin, N. (2022). The future of enterprise and entrepreneurship education in relation to technology. In D. H. Hyams-Ssesaki & N. Yasin (Eds.), *Technology and Entrepreneurship:Adopting Creative Technologies in Entrepreneurship Education*. Palgrave Macmillan/Springer.

Jääskeläinen, M., & Maula, M. (2014). Do networks of financial intermediaries help reduce local bias? Evidence from cross-border venture capital exits. *Journal of Business Venturing, 29*(5), 704–721. https://doi.org/10.1016/j.jbusvent.2013.09.001

Li, Y., & Zahra, S. A. (2012). Formal institutions, culture, and venture capital activity: A cross-country analysis. *Journal of Business Venturing, 27*(1), 95–111. https://doi.org/10.1016/j.jbusvent.2010.06.003

Mason, C., Botelho, T., & Duggett, J. (2022). Promoting cross-border investing by business angels in the European Union. *Regional Studies, 56*(8), 1391–1403. https://doi.org/10.1080/00343404.2021.1960961

Mason, C., & Stark, M. (2004). What do investors look for in a business plan? A comparison of the investment criteria of bankers, venture capitalists, and business angels. *International Small Business Journal, 22*(3), 227–248. https://doi.org/10.1177/0266242604042377

Mestwerdt, S., Mrożewski, M., Sydow, A., & Burkert, N. (2025). Unveiling signaling processes in early-stage cross-border investment: Evidence from south African entrepreneurs and European business angels. *Journal of World Business, 60*(5), 101662. https://doi.org/10.1016/j.jwb.2025.101662

Park, S., & Tuxhorn, K.-L. (2025). Investment across borders: How diaspora firms weigh financial returns and emotional-social drivers. *Asian and Pacific Migration Journal, 34*(4), 653–675. https://doi.org/10.1177/01171968251393548

Paul, S., & Whittam, G. (2010). Business angel syndicates: An exploratory study of gatekeepers. *Venture Capital, 12*(3), 241–256. https://doi.org/10.1080/13691061003711438

Riddle, L., Hrivnak, G. A., & Nielsen, T. M. (2010). Transnational diaspora entrepreneurship in emerging markets: Bridging institutional divides. *Journal of International Management, 16*(4), 398–411. https://doi.org/10.1016/j.intman.2010.09.009

Wesemann, H., & Antretter, T. (2023). The internationalization of business angel networks: Do syndicates increase cross-border investment returns? *Venture Capital, 25*(4), 487–514. https://doi.org/10.1080/13691066.2022.2082898

Yasin, N. (2022). Cold grass or hot sands: A comparative study of immigrant Punjabi-Pakistani entrepreneurs in London and Dubai. *Strategic Change: Briefings in Entrepreneurial Finance, 31*(4), 1–10.

Yasin, N., & Gilani, S. A. M. (2022). 'Imitate or incubate?' evaluating the current state of university-based business incubators in The United Arab Emirates. FIIB business. *Review*. https://doi.org/10.1177/23197145221112744

Yasin, N., & Khansari, Z. (2021a). Evaluating the impact of social enterprise education on students' enterprising characteristics in The United Arab Emirates. *Education + Training, 63*(6), 827–905.

Yasin, N., Gilani, S. A. M., Nair, G., Abaido, G. M., & Askri, S. (2023a). Establishing a nexus for effective university-industry collaborations in the MENA region: A multi-country comparative study. *Industry and Higher Education*. https://doi.org/10.1177/09504222231175862

Yasin, N., & Hafeez, K. (2023). Three waves of immigrant entrepreneurship: A cross-national comparative study. *Small Business Economics, 60*(1), 1281–1306. https://doi.org/10.1007/s11187-022-0065z

Yasin, N., Hafeez, K., & Salamzadeh, A. (2024a). A cross-country comparative ethnographic analysis of immigrant enclave entrepreneurship. *Qualitative Market Research: An International Journal, 28*(1), 1–37. https://doi.org/10.1108/QMR-11-2023-0164

Yasin, N., Haq, M., Dana, L. P., & Salamzadeh, A. (2025a). "Try to keep them dumb and under the thumb": Exploring the darker side of psychological contracts in overly embedded immigrant enterprises. *Employee Relations, 47*(3/4), 537–556. https://doi.org/10.1108/ER-04-2024-0235

Yasin, N., Haq, M., Hafeez, K., & Zahoor, N. (2025b). Are some immigrant entrepreneurs more privileged than others? A cross-national comparison of financial capital among start-ups in the UK and UAE. *The Journal of Race, Ethnicity, and Politics, 1–24*. https://doi.org/10.1017/rep.2025.10031

Yasin, N., & Poulin, M. (2025). Developing a nation of entrepreneurs: The integral role of immigrant entrepreneurship for The United Arab Emirates vision 2030. In C. Margaça, A. Walmsley, & H. Knörr (Eds.), *Immigrant entrepreneurship, religion, and ethnicity: Cases from Europe, Africa, and Asia* (pp. 187–204). Routledge. https://doi.org/10.4324/9781003489214-12

Yasin, N., Margaça, C., Haq, M., Poulin, M., & Salamzadeh, A. (2026b). The multi-capital playbook: Explaining immigrant entrepreneurship through the forms of capital. In C. Salloum, L.-P. Dana, A. Hasnaoui, & M. Rossi (Eds.), *The immigrant Entrepreneur's capital playbook: Green money, global talent, and the path to prosperity*. Springer Nature. Chapter 1.

Yasin, N., & Nabi, G. (2026a). Entrepreneurship education in The United Arab Emirates: An extended resource-based view of institutional resources and contextual challenges in higher education. *International Journal of Entrepreneurial Behaviour and Research*. https://doi.org/10.1108/IJEBR-02-2025-0161

Yasin, N., Hafeez, K., Haq, M., Haq, F., Zahoor, N., & Noaman, S. (2026a). Take a break: A typology of immigrant enterprise growth strategies in non-traditional entrepreneurship settings. *Journal of Entrepreneurship in Emerging Economies*. https://doi.org/10.1108/JEEE-09-2025-0568

Yasin, N. (2013). Broken out and bust: Ayub khan clothing ltd. *Asian Journal of Management Cases, 10*(1), 7–14.

Yasin, N., & Khansari, Z. (2021b). Evaluating the impact of social enterprise education on students' enterprising characteristics in The United Arab Emirates. *Education + Training, 63*(6), 827–905.

Yasin, N., & Gilani, S. A. M. (2022a). 'Imitate or incubate?' evaluating the current state of university-based business incubators in The United Arab Emirates. FIIB business. *Review*. https://doi.org/10.1177/23197145221112744

Yasin, N., & Gilani, S. A. M. (2022b). Assessing the current state of university-based business incubators in Canada. *Industry and Higher Education*. https://doi.org/10.1177/09504222221124749

Yasin, N., & Khansari, Z. (2022). Exploring the enterprise landscape for business incubators in the UAE. In D. Hyams-Ssekasi & F. Agboma (Eds.), *Entrepreneurship and change*. Palgrave Macmillan.

Yasin, N., Gilani, S. A. M., Contu, D., & Fayaz, M. J. (2022). Simulation-based learning in business and entrepreneurship in higher education. In D. Hyams-Ssekasi & N. Yasin (Eds.), *Technology and entrepreneurship: Adopting creative technologies in entrepreneurship education*. Palgrave Macmillan.

Yasin, N., Gilani, S. A. M., Nair, G., Abaido, G. M., & Askri, S. (2023b). Establishing a nexus for effective university-industry collaborations in the MENA region: A multi-country comparative study. *Industry and Higher Education*. https://doi.org/10.1177/09504222231175862

Yasin, N., Noaman, S., Gilani, S. A. M., & Askari, S. (2024b). Revolutionising fitness on the go! A case study of MAXPRO fitness. *Asian Journal of Management Cases*. https://doi.org/10.1177/09728201241271501

Yasin, N., & Nabi, G. (2026b). Entrepreneurship education in The United Arab Emirates: An extended resource-based view of institutional resources and contextual challenges in higher education. *International Journal of Entrepreneurial Behaviour and Research*. https://doi.org/10.1108/IJEBR-02-2025-0161

Valuation Under Uncertainty in Thin Markets: Tickets, Tranches, and Exit Discipline for Diaspora Angels

Jean-Michel Sahut

Abstract This chapter examines how diaspora angels approach valuation when price discovery is weak, exits are uncertain, and comparable transactions are sparse. It does not introduce a new valuation model. Instead, it consolidates evidence from the angel-investing, international entrepreneurship, and diaspora-investment literatures to show that valuation in thin markets is less a single number than a disciplined sequence of judgments. The analysis explains why investors rely more heavily on network-based due diligence, milestone finance, co-investor validation, and exit realism than on spreadsheet precision alone. It also shows how diaspora ties can reduce informational opacity without cancelling institutional risk. By connecting evidence on cross-border signalling, trust, and syndication to investor practice, the chapter offers a mature framework for setting ticket size, tranche conditions, and downside protection in uneven ecosystems. The result is a practical, evidence-based approach to pricing early-stage deals when markets do not provide clean benchmarks.

1 Introduction

In early-stage finance, valuation is often presented as a technical exercise. In thick markets that simplification is already imperfect. In thin markets it becomes misleading. Founders and investors are not merely estimating future cash flows; they are pricing uncertainty under weak institutional support, sparse comparables, and ambiguous exit routes. A startup in Accra, Kigali, Tbilisi, or Sarajevo may have real commercial promise and still offer little that resembles the information environment assumed by standard valuation tools. What investors face, then, is not just risk. They face noisy signals, thin evidence, and an unusually high cost of being wrong (Alemany & Andreoli, 2026; Edelman et al., 2017).

That difficulty becomes sharper in cross-border settings. Early-stage collaboration between founders and investors from different countries is shaped by distance, weak verifiability, and contextual misunderstanding. Mestwerdt et al. (2025) show that in

J.-M. Sahut (✉)
IDRAC Business School, Lyon, France
e-mail: jeanmichel.sahut@idrac-bs.fr

H. Jarrar et al. (eds.), *Diaspora Angel Investing*, Ethnic and Indigenous Business Studies, https://doi.org/10.1007/978-3-032-33088-8_4

such settings information asymmetry is not a side issue. It sits at the centre of the relationship and influences how even credible signals are interpreted. Lerner et al. (2018) likewise show that angel investment has become increasingly international, which makes the problem more important rather than less. As cross-border angel activity expands, valuation cannot be treated as if all ecosystems produce comparable information at comparable cost.

Diaspora investors matter here because they are not ordinary foreign investors. Their dual embeddedness gives them unusual access to language, norms, informal networks, and local credibility, allowing them to bridge institutional divides that would otherwise discourage investment (Riddle et al., 2010; Stoyanov et al., 2018). Dizo-Conteh et al. (2025) show this clearly in the SME internationalization context: diaspora networks help transfer market knowledge, validate counterparties, and reduce friction around institutional voids. Yet familiarity has limits. Park and Tuxhorn (2025) find that emotional and social motivations support homeland investment only when the economic case remains credible. This chapter therefore treats valuation as a disciplined synthesis of financial judgment, contextual interpretation, and deal design. The aim is practical. It clarifies how diaspora angels can price early-stage opportunities in thin markets without drifting into sentiment-driven overvaluation.

There is a second reason this matters. In thin markets, valuation errors reverberate longer because corrective market signals arrive slowly. An inflated entry price can poison the next round if later investors refuse to inherit assumptions that were never properly tested. An excessively low price can be just as damaging, especially when it dilutes founders so early that later incentives weaken or the best entrepreneurs simply avoid diaspora capital altogether. Good valuation therefore protects both sides. It preserves founder credibility for future rounds and investor credibility for future participation. In practice, the most respected diaspora investors are rarely the ones who paid the highest initial prices. They are the ones whose pricing proved durable once outside capital looked at the company.

This chapter contributes to the investor-side playbook of the volume by showing how diaspora angels can translate network familiarity into pricing discipline, staged capital, syndicate validation, downside protection, and exit-aware term design. It treats valuation not as a single number, but as a governance process that determines how trust, uncertainty, and future optionality are allocated between founder and investor.

2 Repricing Uncertainty When the Market Gives Little Guidance

Thin markets do not eliminate valuation. They change what valuation has to do. In a dense market, investors can benchmark a deal against recent rounds, known acquirers, familiar term structures, and a visible pipeline of follow-on capital. In a thin market, none of that can be taken for granted. The immediate consequence is that a spreadsheet-based valuation often looks more precise than the environment warrants. Revenue forecasts may be built on untested customer segments. Cost assumptions may ignore logistics, foreign exchange volatility, or regulatory delay. Exit multiples may come from markets with deeper buyer pools and stronger disclosure norms than the target firm will ever face. The problem is not that formal methods are useless. It is that their inputs are unstable and the error bars are much wider than the final number suggests (Alemany & Andreoli, 2026; Mustafa, 2021).

Cross-border evidence reinforces this point. Hain et al. (2016) show that relational and institutional trust significantly shape cross-border venture investment patterns, especially when investors are moving across environments with different governance conditions. Li and Zahra (2012) similarly demonstrate that formal institutions and culture affect the level and character of venture-capital activity across countries. Once these institutional effects are acknowledged, valuation can no longer be framed as a purely venture-specific calculation. It becomes a layered judgment involving venture quality, contextual reliability, and the investor's capacity to monitor and support the company after the round closes.

Another angle matters here. Thin markets often collapse three different risks into a single discount. Investors see weak accounting, uncertain regulation, and fragile exit routes, then respond by simply lowering price. Sometimes that is sensible. Often it is crude. Venture risk concerns the product, team, and business model. Context risk concerns contract enforcement, information reliability, currency exposure, and market depth. Execution risk concerns whether the investor and founder can work effectively across borders and whether follow-on capital will be available when needed. Treating all three as one blunt number leads to either inflated optimism or excessive discounting. The better approach is to disaggregate the problem. Once the investor knows which uncertainty comes from the company and which comes from the environment, price discipline improves.

This is where diaspora investors can make a genuine difference, though not a magical one. Leblang (2010) and Tong (2005) show that diaspora and ethnic networks influence cross-border investment because familiarity lowers search and monitoring costs. The value of that familiarity is not that it makes every deal safe. It makes certain risks legible. A diaspora investor may understand whether a founder's claimed distribution partner is real, whether a local regulator is likely to delay approval, or whether a prospective customer base is genuinely reachable. That knowledge should narrow uncertainty, not inflate valuation. In practice, the best diaspora investors use familiarity to refine the discount rate conceptually, even if they never calculate one formally. They are better at distinguishing opacity from opportunity.

A practical habit follows from this. Instead of defending a point estimate too early, disciplined investors often work with a valuation range anchored in explicit assumptions. The lower bound reflects the current evidence set, the upper bound reflects what could reasonably be defended if a few identified uncertainties resolve well, and the actual deal is then structured so that further evidence can move the company from one bound toward the other. This range-based logic is especially helpful in countries where historical deal data are either too sparse or too distorted by idiosyncratic transactions to function as clean comparables. It also reduces the temptation to use one celebrated outlier round as proof that the whole ecosystem has repriced.

Underpricing can be as distorting as overpricing. When investors apply a blanket "country discount" without asking which part of the risk can actually be reduced through structure or network support, they often end up buying too much ownership too early. The short-term logic seems prudent, yet the longer-term effect can be adverse selection: stronger founders avoid the capital source, while weaker firms accept it because they have no alternative. Over time, that pattern reinforces the idea that the market only produces low-quality opportunities. A disciplined valuation process avoids that trap by distinguishing between risks that deserve a lower price now and risks that can be handled through milestones, governance, and investor support.

3 Diaspora Investors as Signal Interpreters, Not Just Capital Providers

Much of early-stage valuation rests on signals. Founders signal quality through prior achievements, customer traction, technical credibility, and the company they keep. Investors signal value through their reputation, monitoring capacity, and willingness to lead. In thick markets, these signals are easier to compare because the surrounding institutions translate them into relatively stable meanings. In thin markets, the same signal can be misread. Mestwerdt et al. (2025) show that in cross-border angel investment, contextual biases can lead to signal appreciation, signal depreciation, or even signal flip, where one party's intended message is interpreted in the opposite way. That finding is especially important for diaspora angels. Their edge lies not only in seeing more signals, but in reading them with more context.

Dizo-Conteh et al. (2025) provide complementary evidence. Their study of diaspora networks and SME internationalization shows that diaspora actors bridge institutional voids by transferring market-specific knowledge, expanding network access, and enhancing credibility. In valuation terms, that means certain uncertainties can be checked against lived knowledge rather than generic country templates. A diaspora investor may know which hospital system in a healthcare market actually pays on time, which export broker has a real record, or which founder's family reputation carries weight in a way outside investors would miss. Stoyanov et al. (2018) describe this as leveraging the assets of foreignness through diaspora embedding. The important point is practical: diaspora proximity can improve the quality of valuation inputs even when it does not change the structure of the model itself.

Still, diaspora affiliation should never be treated as a valuation premium in its own right. Park and Tuxhorn (2025) offer a useful warning. Their evidence from Korean diaspora firms shows that non-material motivations encourage homeland investment when expected returns are broadly comparable, but do not compensate for a clearly inferior financial proposition. The implication is straightforward. Emotional attachment may expand the set of deals an investor is willing to examine. It should not justify paying a price unsupported by expected outcomes. Homeland affinity can open the door. It should not rewrite basic economics.

The most reliable signals in thin markets are usually those that travel across contexts. Verified recurring revenue matters more than social visibility. A signed export contract is stronger than local buzz. Evidence that a product already works with paying diaspora customers abroad can be more informative than optimistic total-addressable-market claims. Co-investment with a trusted lead, independent technical diligence, clean intellectual-property ownership, and traceable use of proceeds are also powerful because they reduce the cost of interpretation. What matters here is that valuation improves when the investor asks not only whether a signal is positive, but whether it remains credible after it leaves its local context. Diaspora investors are unusually well positioned to test that question. Their advantage is interpretive discipline.

One useful discipline is to sort evidence into three buckets before discussing price. Hard signals include banked revenue, signed contracts, audited accounts, regulatory approvals, and cap-table clarity. Relational signals include trusted referrals, founder reputation in the diaspora community, and validation from experienced operators. Contextual signals include evidence about market access, payment practices, hiring realities, and procurement behavior in the country itself. Founders usually present all three at once, which is understandable. Investors make better pricing decisions when they keep the categories separate. Hard signals can justify immediate confidence. Relational signals can justify deeper diligence. Contextual signals can justify how much patience or discount the deal deserves. The distinction sounds basic, yet in thin markets it prevents many avoidable pricing mistakes.

Founders benefit from this logic as much as investors do. When the evidence package is organized well, the company can tell a stronger financing story to future co-investors and later-stage funds. In thin markets, many companies lose credibility not because their businesses are weak, but because their diligence materials mix aspiration, community endorsement, and operating evidence in ways that outsiders struggle to parse. Diaspora angels who insist on cleaner signalling are therefore not merely protecting themselves. They are helping the venture become financeable on broader terms later.

4 Tickets, Tranches, and Downside Protection

In thin markets, the smartest valuation move is often not to win an argument over the headline price. It is to reduce the cost of being early. When comparables are scarce, follow-on capital is uncertain, and market feedback is noisy, committing a large amount at a single fixed valuation can create avoidable risk for both investor and founder. Mustafa (2021) shows, in the Indian angel market, that early-stage investing depends heavily on how investors pace commitment, support founders, and preserve optionality. Edelman et al. (2017) similarly emphasize that angel investing is characterized by uncertainty, incomplete contracting, and ongoing involvement. Under these conditions, price is only one element of discipline. Ticket size, tranche design, monitoring rights, reserve planning, and term-sheet structure are just as important.

A smaller initial ticket can be more rational than forcing a definitive valuation too early. It allows the investor to test the quality of the evidence without overcommitting capital before uncertainty is reduced. It also protects the founder from excessive dilution at a point when the company has not yet demonstrated enough commercial traction to defend a higher price. In thin markets, the issue is rarely whether the opportunity is promising. The issue is whether the next informative event is sufficiently clear to justify more capital later. Good diaspora investors therefore ask a simple question before debating valuation: what evidence would make this company genuinely more valuable six or twelve months from now?

Milestone-based staging answers that question directly. The first tranche may finance product completion, regulatory clearance, first paying customers, export activation, or operational reliability. A second tranche may be released only after verified monthly recurring revenue, customer retention, signed procurement, institutional approval, or gross-margin discipline. This approach protects the investor against premature overexposure and protects the founder from being locked into a weak valuation for longer than necessary. Staging works best when milestones are observable, commercial, and difficult to manipulate. Cash collection, retention, signed contracts, regulatory approvals, and repeat usage travel better across borders than press coverage, downloads, or vague partnership announcements.

Instrument choice should also reflect the quality of future price discovery. Convertible notes or SAFEs can be attractive because they postpone the hardest valuation discussion. In thin markets, however, deferral is useful only if a later priced round is plausible and likely to be led by investors with a stronger information set. If that future round is uncertain, a deferral instrument may simply hide today's valuation problem and create tomorrow's dilution conflict. Priced equity with staged capital can be cleaner when investors expect to remain close to the company and when milestone evidence can be generated without waiting for a distant lead investor to certify the business.

Downside protection should be handled with balance. Thin markets do not justify predatory terms. They do justify clarity. Information rights, pro rata rights, reserved matters, board observation, liquidation preferences, milestone release conditions, and ESG covenants can preserve investor discipline without suffocating the business. The best arrangements match protection to the source of uncertainty. If the main concern is information quality, reporting rights matter most. If the concern is follow-on dilution, pro rata rights are more relevant. If the concern is governance drift, reserved matters or board observation may be appropriate. If the concern is impact-washing, reporting covenants and measurable ESG indicators are more useful than a vague sustainability premium (Table 1).

Syndication strengthens this term-sheet logic. Mason et al. (2022) show that cross-border angel investing faces predictable constraints around information, networks, and institutional fragmentation. A syndicate can spread diligence costs, improve

Table 1 From valuation problem to term-sheet response

Valuation problem	Term-sheet response	Practical discipline
Weak information quality	Information rights, monthly reporting, access to management accounts	Do not price on narrative alone
Follow-on uncertainty	Staged tranches, milestone-based release, investor reserve planning	Avoid overcommitting too early
Exit uncertainty	Liquidation preference, exit consultation rights, realistic exit map	Protect downside without suffocating the firm
Founder dilution risk	Smaller initial ticket, founder-friendly option pool, staged valuation adjustment	Avoid weakening future incentives
Governance drift	Reserved matters, board observer, consent rights for major decisions	Match control to actual risk
Currency or transfer risk	Local-currency provisions, FX adjustment logic, clear remittance terms	Avoid hidden valuation erosion
Syndicate fragmentation	Syndicate SPV, lead investor rights, pro rata rules, standardised reporting	Reduce coordination costs among diaspora angels
ESG or climate claim	ESG covenant, use-of-proceeds reporting, impact KPI	Prevent impact-washing and valuation inflation

Source Author's own elaboration

sector expertise, and increase the probability of follow-on support. Wesemann and Antretter (2023) add that larger cross-border syndicates are less sensitive to geographic and cultural distance and can achieve stronger returns. For diaspora angels, syndication is therefore not only a risk-sharing device. It is a valuation tool. A company backed by a credible syndicate may deserve a narrower risk discount than the same company financed by an isolated investor, because the syndicate improves monitoring, support, signaling, and future financing credibility.

In diaspora settings, syndicate SPVs can solve an additional coordination problem. Many diaspora angels invest relatively small tickets, often across geographies, and with uneven capacity to monitor the company directly. A syndicate SPV can pool commitments, simplify the cap table, designate a lead investor, standardize information rights, coordinate tranche release, and give the founder one organized counterparty rather than many fragmented small investors. The structure is not merely administrative. It can improve valuation discipline because one lead investor can coordinate diligence, negotiate protections, manage follow-on decisions, and represent the syndicate in exit discussions.

For climate-enabling or impact-oriented ventures, diaspora angels should also apply a simple ESG screen before accepting any valuation premium. The screen should ask whether the environmental or social claim is material to the business model, whether the venture can report at least one credible impact indicator, whether labor and governance risks are controlled, and whether the claimed impact survives outside the founder's narrative. This prevents climate language, homeland attachment, or community pride from becoming another source of overvaluation. A sustainability claim can strengthen a deal only when it is measurable, commercially relevant, and governable.

Box 1: Sample Term-Sheet Language for Milestone Tranches

"The investment shall be disbursed in two tranches. The first tranche of [amount] shall be released at closing. The second tranche of [amount] shall be released upon verification by the lead investor that the company has achieved [defined commercial milestone], including [evidence standard]. If the milestone is not achieved by [date], the parties shall review the valuation, use of proceeds, and financing plan before any further disbursement."

The practical logic can be summarized as follows. In thin markets, valuation should be converted into disciplined pacing. A lower initial exposure, credible milestones, syndicate coordination, proportionate downside protection, and a simple ESG screen can produce better investment decisions than a fragile debate over a single pre-money number. Good valuation is therefore not only about price. It is about designing a transaction that allows better evidence to emerge before more capital is committed (Table 2).

Table 2 Illustrative milestone packages for staged valuation

Venture profile	Milestone 1	Milestone 2	Likely valuation effect
Exportable software	Working product and three paying clients	Retention and repeat revenue established	Supports a tighter follow-on pricing range
Healthcare service or medtech	Regulatory or institutional clearance	Contracted demand from credible buyers	Justifies release of later tranches
Marketplace or logistics platform	Verified transaction quality and gross margin visibility	Repeat usage and operational reliability	Reduces narrative-heavy pricing
Climate-enabling B2B venture	Paid pilot converted from demonstration	Evidence of repeat procurement	Improves confidence in a longer exit path
Consumer venture in a local market	Evidence of repeat paying demand and contribution margin	Channel reliability and cash collection discipline	Keeps price grounded when exits are narrow
Asset-heavy or hardware venture	Prototype reliability and procurement visibility	Working-capital discipline and delivery execution	Signals whether later capital needs will distort entry valuation

Source Author's own elaboration based on Mustafa (2021),Edelman et al. (2017)

5 Exit Discipline and Hybrid Comparables

Every early-stage valuation contains an implicit exit story. In thick markets that story may be left unstated because later rounds, active acquirers, or public markets make several routes plausible. Thin markets are less forgiving. If there are few active buyers, shallow domestic capital markets, and uncertain follow-on investors, exit cannot be treated as a distant detail. It has to shape entry discipline from the start. Angel investors have long screened deals with exit in mind, and that habit becomes more important when the local market cannot absorb many late-stage outcomes (Edelman et al., 2017).

A frequent mistake is to import comparables from ecosystems with very different exit conditions. A health-tech company in Nairobi should not be priced as if it will exit on the same timeline and at the same multiple as a peer in Boston. At the same time, using only local benchmarks can be equally distorting when the local market is too thin to generate meaningful comparables. The more credible approach is hybrid. The investor starts with sector benchmarks from the most plausible acquisition or later-stage capital market, then adjusts them for governance quality, foreign-exchange exposure, market access, and time-to-exit. This is slower than applying a simple multiple, but it is also less misleading. It forces the investor to ask who would realistically buy this company, from which jurisdiction, and under what governance conditions.

Intermediary networks matter at this stage as well. Jääskeläinen and Maula (2014) show that networks of financial intermediaries can reduce local bias in cross-border venture-capital exits. The implication for diaspora angels is straightforward: exit probability is not just a property of the portfolio company. It is shaped by the investor's network reach. A diaspora-led syndicate with credible ties to later-stage investors, strategic buyers, and foreign commercial partners may reasonably accept a tighter entry discount than an isolated angel investing alone. That is not because the company itself is less risky. It is because the path from seed stage to liquid outcome is more visible.

This also explains why sector choice matters. Some sectors travel better than others. Exportable software, B2B infrastructure, healthcare services with transferable know-how, and climate-enabling technologies may connect naturally to regional or global buyer pools. Other sectors remain heavily local and therefore depend more on domestic capital depth, which many thin markets still lack. Dizo-Conteh et al. (2025) show how diaspora networks can support cross-border product adaptation and market access, especially in knowledge-intensive sectors. That type of access can change the exit map meaningfully. By contrast, a consumer startup whose economics depend almost entirely on a narrow local market may remain difficult to price generously no matter how compelling the narrative sounds.

Valuation discipline improves when investors begin with the most plausible exit universe, not the most flattering one. In practice, that usually produces a range rather than a single heroic number. The range narrows only as evidence accumulates and the route to follow-on capital becomes clearer. Thin markets reward investors who can hold that tension. They neither underprice everything because exits are hard, nor accept inflated pricing because the founder's story is attractive. They price to the exit they can actually imagine reaching.

The exit map should also be written down, not left implicit. A disciplined diaspora investor will usually identify at least three plausible routes: a local or regional strategic buyer, a later-stage foreign investor, and a cross-border buyer already connected to the sector through trade, technology, or distribution. Each route implies a different timeline, governance threshold, and valuation ceiling. Writing these routes down forces the investor to confront awkward but useful questions. Which of these buyers would tolerate local governance gaps? Which would insist on redomiciliation or stronger reporting? Which would care more about customer concentration than growth? Once these questions are asked early, entry valuation becomes more realistic and post-investment support becomes more focused.

There is a practical portfolio implication here as well. Diaspora angels often invest in more than one corridor or sector over time, which means they can compare exits across contexts from lived experience rather than from theory alone. When

Table 3 Evidence-based valuation responses in thin markets

Valuation problem	What often goes wrong	Better response	Why it matters
Sparse comparables	Foreign multiples are copied without adjustment	Use hybrid comparables and adjust for governance, liquidity, and time-to-exit	Prevents imported overvaluation
Weak signal quality	Narrative strength is mistaken for commercial proof	Prioritize verifiable traction, contracts, and independent validation	Improves the quality of pricing inputs
High uncertainty at entry	A single price is forced too early	Use smaller tickets and milestone tranches	Protects capital while allowing repricing
Limited exit routes	Entry valuation ignores buyer reality	Map the most plausible exit universe before pricing	Aligns entry price with realizable outcomes
Context risk bundled into venture risk	Country conditions are discounted without diagnosis	Separate venture, context, and execution risk before pricing	Produces cleaner negotiation and better term design
Homeland familiarity treated as price premium	Emotional proximity overrides evidence	Use diaspora knowledge to sharpen diligence, not justify overpayment	Keeps identity from distorting economics

Source Author's own elaboration based on Alemany and Andreoli (2026), Edelman et al. (2017), Mason et al. (2022), andMestwerdt et al. (2025)

these investors document why one exit route worked and another failed, they create internal benchmarks that are often more useful than broad market multiples. Over several deals, those benchmarks become a private knowledge asset. They allow the investor to price new opportunities with greater realism because the exit map is informed by actual comparable journeys, not just headline valuations from unrelated ecosystems (Table 3).

6 Conclusion

Valuation in thin markets is best understood as a governance problem with financial consequences. The central question is not whether a model can produce a number, but whether the investor can defend that number once institutional friction, signal distortion, weak comparables, currency exposure, syndicate coordination, and exit uncertainty are made explicit. In these environments, valuation is not a one-off calculation. It is a disciplined sequence of judgments about what is known, what remains uncertain, which risks can be priced immediately, and which risks should instead be managed through tranches, milestones, syndication, information rights, downside protection, and exit planning.

Diaspora angels hold a specific advantage in this process because they can reduce informational opacity through language, familiarity, trust, and network embeddedness. They may understand local reputation, payment practices, institutional bottlenecks, procurement realities, and founder credibility in ways that ordinary foreign investors cannot. However, this advantage should sharpen diligence, not inflate price. Diaspora familiarity is valuable because it makes certain risks more legible; it does not remove institutional risk, execution risk, or exit risk. Emotional attachment, homeland loyalty, and community pride can expand the set of deals an investor is willing to examine, but they should not justify a valuation that cannot be defended by evidence, milestones, or plausible exit routes.

The chapter therefore recommends that diaspora angels begin valuation with risk disaggregation. Venture risk, context risk, execution risk, currency risk, governance risk, and exit risk should not be collapsed into one blunt "country discount". Some risks deserve a lower entry valuation. Others are better handled through structure. Weak information quality calls for reporting rights, access to management accounts, and external validation. Follow-on uncertainty calls for smaller initial tickets, investor reserve planning, and milestone-based tranches. Governance drift calls for reserved matters, board observation, or consent rights. Syndicate fragmentation calls for a lead investor, standardized reporting, pro rata rules, or a syndicate SPV. ESG or climate claims call for measurable impact indicators, use-of-proceeds reporting, and safeguards against impact-washing.

A second recommendation is to treat ticket size and tranche design as part of valuation rather than as secondary deal mechanics. In thin markets, the most disciplined investor is not necessarily the one who negotiates the lowest price. It is the one who commits the right amount of capital at the right moment, tied to the next informative milestone. A small initial ticket can preserve optionality, reduce premature dilution, and create space for evidence to emerge. Tranches should be linked to observable commercial events: paying customers, retention, signed contracts, regulatory approvals, gross-margin visibility, working-capital discipline, or repeat procurement. Vague milestones based on visibility, enthusiasm, downloads, or informal endorsements should not trigger repricing or capital release.

A third recommendation is to use syndication deliberately. Cross-border diaspora investing often involves many small investors with uneven monitoring capacity. Without coordination, this can fragment the cap table and weaken governance. A syndicate SPV can pool capital, designate a lead investor, simplify communication with the founder, standardize information rights, coordinate follow-on decisions, and represent the investor group in exit negotiations. This improves valuation discipline because one organized counterparty can translate dispersed diaspora interest into coherent diligence, pricing, monitoring, and support. For founders, this can also be beneficial: a clean syndicate structure is more attractive to future institutional investors than a crowded cap table of small, uncoordinated angels.

A fourth recommendation is to make exit discipline explicit before investing. In thin markets, entry valuation should be linked to the most plausible exit universe, not to the most flattering comparable. Investors should write down at least three possible routes: a local or regional strategic buyer, a later-stage foreign investor, and a cross-border acquirer connected to the sector through trade, technology, healthcare, climate, logistics, or distribution. Each route implies a different timeline, governance threshold, reporting requirement, and valuation ceiling. This exercise prevents imported overvaluation from deeper markets and avoids the opposite mistake of applying excessive local discounts where diaspora networks may genuinely expand the exit map.

A fifth recommendation concerns ESG and climate-enabling ventures. Diaspora investors should not pay an impact premium unless the environmental or social claim is material to the business model, measurable through at least one credible indicator, and supported by governance controls. Climate language, homeland development narratives, and community benefit claims can strengthen a deal only when they survive diligence outside the founder's story. A simple ESG screen should therefore ask whether the venture controls labor, governance, environmental, and impact-reporting risks, and whether sustainability improves commercial resilience rather than merely decorating the pitch.

For founders, the implication is equally clear. A stronger valuation story does not come from optimism alone. It comes from organized evidence. Founders seeking diaspora capital should separate hard signals, relational signals, and contextual signals. Banked revenue, signed contracts, regulatory approvals, and clean cap tables should be distinguished from community endorsement, trusted referrals, or market narratives. This discipline helps diaspora angels price the deal more fairly and helps the venture become financeable by later-stage or non-diaspora investors.

For ecosystems, valuation discipline has wider consequences. When diaspora angels price deals on evidence rather than excitement, they do more than protect individual portfolios. They create better reference points for future founders, future syndicates, and future outside investors. Thin markets improve when early prices reflect credible information, realistic milestones, proportionate protections, and plausible exits. Poorly disciplined valuations, by contrast, can damage entire corridors by creating down-rounds, founder distrust, cap-table problems, and scepticism among later investors.

The broader contribution of this chapter is therefore to reposition diaspora angel valuation as a form of market-building. Diaspora investors can mobilize global networks for local impact, but only if familiarity is converted into disciplined pricing, staged capital, syndicate governance, ESG accountability, and exit realism. The practical test is simple: can the valuation still be defended when the emotional appeal of the deal is removed and only evidence, structure, and exit logic remain? If the answer is yes, diaspora capital can cross borders without losing judgment on the way.

References

Alemany, L., & Andreoli, J. J. (Eds.). (2026). *Entrepreneurial finance: The art and science of growing ventures* (2nd ed.). Cambridge University Press. https://doi.org/10.1017/9781009537827

Dizo-Conteh, U., Tasavori, M., & Afrahi, B. (2025). The contribution of diaspora networks to the internationalisation of SMEs: A case study in the healthcare industry. *Journal of International Management, 31*(6), Article 101306. https://doi.org/10.1016/j.intman.2025.101306

Edelman, L. F., Manolova, T. S., & Brush, C. G. (2017). Angel investing: A literature review. *Foundations and Trends in Entrepreneurship, 13*(4–5), 265–439. https://doi.org/10.1561/0300000051

Hain, D., Johan, S. A., & Wang, D. (2016). Determinants of cross-border venture capital investments in emerging and developed economies: The effects of relational and institutional trust. *Journal of Business Ethics, 138*(4), 743–764. https://doi.org/10.1007/s10551-015-2772-4

Jääskeläinen, M., & Maula, M. (2014). Do networks of financial intermediaries help reduce local bias? Evidence from cross-border venture capital exits. *Journal of Business Venturing, 29*(5), 704–721. https://doi.org/10.1016/j.jbusvent.2013.09.001

Leblang, D. (2010). Familiarity breeds investment: Diaspora networks and international investment. *American Political Science Review, 104*(3), 584–600. https://doi.org/10.1017/S0003055410000201

Lerner, J., Schoar, A., Sokolinski, S., & Wilson, K. (2018). The globalization of angel investments: Evidence across countries. *Journal of Financial Economics, 127*(1), 1–20. https://doi.org/10.1016/j.jfineco.2017.05.012

Li, Y., & Zahra, S. A. (2012). Formal institutions, culture, and venture capital activity: A cross-country analysis. *Journal of Business Venturing, 27*(1), 95–111. https://doi.org/10.1016/j.jbusvent.2010.06.003

Mason, C., Botelho, T., & Duggett, J. (2022). Promoting cross-border investing by business angels in the European Union. *Regional Studies, 56*(8), 1391–1403. https://doi.org/10.1080/00343404.2021.1960961

Mestwerdt, S., Mrożewski, M., Sydow, A., & Burkert, N. (2025). Unveiling signaling processes in early-stage cross-border investment: Evidence from South African entrepreneurs and European business angels. *Journal of World Business, 60*(5), Article 101662. https://doi.org/10.1016/j.jwb.2025.101662

Mustafa, M. (2021). *Angel investing: The untold story of India*. Palgrave Macmillan. https://doi.org/10.1007/978-981-16-0921-3

Park, S., & Tuxhorn, K.-L. (2025). Investment across borders: How diaspora firms weigh financial returns and emotional-social drivers. *Asian and Pacific Migration Journal, 34*(4), 653–675. https://doi.org/10.1177/01171968251393548

Riddle, L., Hrivnak, G. A., & Nielsen, T. M. (2010). Transnational diaspora entrepreneurship in emerging markets: Bridging institutional divides. *Journal of International Management, 16*(4), 398–411. https://doi.org/10.1016/j.intman.2010.09.009

Stoyanov, S., Woodward, R., & Stoyanova, V. (2018). The embedding of transnational entrepreneurs in diaspora networks: Leveraging the assets of foreignness. *Management International Review, 58*(2), 281–312. https://doi.org/10.1007/s11575-017-0336-9

Tong, S. Y. (2005). Ethnic networks in FDI and the impact of institutional development. *Review of Development Economics, 9*(4), 563–580. https://doi.org/10.1111/j.1467-9361.2005.00294.x

Wesemann, H., & Antretter, T. (2023). The internationalization of business angel networks: Do syndicates increase cross-border investment returns? *Venture Capital, 25*(4), 487–514. https://doi.org/10.1080/13691066.2022.2082898

Structuring Diaspora Angel Deals: Syndicates, SPVs, and Cross-Border Legal Basics

Jean-Michel Sahut

Abstract This chapter synthesizes established evidence on how diaspora angel deals should be structured when investors, founders, and assets sit across different jurisdictions. Rather than offering jurisdiction-specific legal advice, it distills what the literature on business angels, cross-border finance, and diaspora investment consistently shows about syndication, special-purpose vehicles, and recurring legal frictions. The chapter explains why syndicates reduce information costs, why SPVs can simplify cap-table management while creating new coordination burdens, and why legal basics such as governing law, tax exposure, investor rights, compliance, and intellectual-property ownership can change deal economics more than founders initially expect. It also shows that relational trust must be translated into institutional clarity if diaspora capital is to travel well. The result is a practical, evidence-based framework for structuring cross-border early-stage deals that are both financeable and governable.

1 Introduction

In early-stage finance, valuation is often presented as a technical exercise. In thick markets, that simplification is already imperfect. In thin markets, it becomes misleading. In this chapter, thin markets refer to early-stage investment environments in which comparable transactions are scarce, follow-on capital is uncertain, exit routes are narrow, institutional signals are costly to verify, and standard valuation inputs are unusually unstable. Founders and investors are therefore not merely estimating future cash flows. They are pricing uncertainty under weak institutional support, sparse benchmarks, ambiguous buyer pools, and a high cost of being wrong. A startup in Accra, Kigali, Tbilisi, or Sarajevo may have real commercial promise and still offer little that resembles the information environment assumed by standard valuation tools. In such settings, spreadsheet precision can conceal rather than resolve uncertainty (Alemany & Andreoli, 2026; Edelman et al., 2017).

J.-M. Sahut (✉)
IDRAC Business School, Lyon, France
e-mail: jeanmichel.sahut@idrac-bs.fr

H. Jarrar et al. (eds.), *Diaspora Angel Investing*, Ethnic and Indigenous Business Studies, https://doi.org/10.1007/978-3-032-33088-8_5

The difficulty becomes sharper in cross-border settings. Early-stage collaboration between founders and investors from different countries is shaped by distance, weak verifiability, contextual misunderstanding, and uneven institutional reliability. Mestwerdt et al. (2025) show that information asymmetry is not peripheral in early-stage cross-border investment; it sits at the centre of the relationship and influences how even credible signals are interpreted. Lerner et al. (2018) similarly show that angel investment has become increasingly international, making the problem more important rather than less. As cross-border angel activity expands, valuation cannot be treated as if all ecosystems generate comparable evidence, comparable risks, and comparable exit options at comparable cost.

Diaspora investors matter because they are not ordinary foreign investors. Their dual embeddedness gives them access to language, norms, informal networks, local credibility, and cross-border interpretive capacity, allowing them to bridge institutional divides that would otherwise discourage investment. Dizo-Conteh et al. show this clearly in the SME internationalization context: diaspora networks can transfer market knowledge, validate counterparties, and reduce friction around institutional voids. Yet this advantage should not be romanticized. Park and Tuxhorn find that emotional and social motivations support homeland investment only when the economic case remains credible. Diaspora angels are therefore not valuable because they can ignore uncertainty. They are valuable because they can interpret some uncertainties more accurately, mobilize trusted verification channels, and help founders prepare evidence packages that later-stage investors can understand.

There is a second reason valuation discipline matters. In thin markets, valuation errors reverberate longer because corrective market signals arrive slowly. An inflated entry price can poison the next round if later investors refuse to inherit assumptions that were never properly tested. An excessively low price can also be damaging, especially when early dilution weakens founder incentives or discourages high-quality entrepreneurs from accepting diaspora capital. Good valuation therefore protects both sides. It preserves founder credibility for future rounds and investor credibility for future participation. In practice, the most respected diaspora investors are rarely those who paid the highest initial prices. They are those whose pricing remains defensible once outside capital examines the company.

This chapter contributes to the investor-side playbook of the volume by showing how diaspora angels can translate network familiarity into pricing discipline, staged capital, syndicate validation, downside protection, ESG screening, and exit-aware term design. It treats valuation not as a single number, but as a governance process that determines how trust, uncertainty, and future optionality are allocated between founder and investor. The argument is practical throughout: diaspora capital can travel across borders without losing judgment only when familiarity sharpens diligence, when tickets and tranches allow evidence to emerge, and when valuation is tied to plausible exits rather than sentiment or imported benchmarks.

2 Why Syndication Matters More in Diaspora Deals

Syndication is often described as a way of sharing risk. That is true, but incomplete. In cross-border diaspora investing its first function is information production. A single investor rarely has the sector knowledge, country knowledge, legal reach, and follow-on capacity needed to evaluate a thin-market deal properly. A syndicate creates a division of labor. One member may understand the technology. Another may understand the local customer base. A third may be better placed to judge the legal or accounting environment. The lead investor then turns these pieces into a coherent investment decision.

The evidence supports this logic. Wesemann and Antretter (2023) show that larger syndicates are less sensitive to the costs of geographic and cultural distance in cross-border angel investing and earn stronger returns. Hain et al. (2016) similarly show that relational trust matters for cross-border venture finance, especially when investors move between institutional settings that differ markedly in reliability. Syndication helps transform fragile bilateral trust into a more robust decision process because information can be checked from more than one angle. That is valuable in any market. It is particularly valuable where institutional noise is high.

There is another reason syndication matters. It improves founder selection and post-investment support at the same time. Paul and Whittam (2010) show that angel syndicates often rely on gatekeepers who control access to opportunities and coordinate the screening process. In thin markets, that gatekeeping role can be decisive. A disciplined lead investor can filter out socially attractive but commercially weak opportunities before a broader diaspora group becomes emotionally committed. Once the deal is closed, the same structure makes it easier to allocate board work, customer introductions, operational mentoring, and later-round fundraising support.

That said, not every syndicate adds value. Informal groups with vague leadership, unclear follow-on intentions, or inconsistent risk appetites can make a deal harder rather than easier. Founders then spend more time managing investors than building the company. The practical lesson is simple. A syndicate should exist because it improves the information set, the governance capacity, or the follow-on pathway. It should not exist merely because several investors wish to be associated with the deal. In diaspora settings, that distinction is crucial. Community visibility is not the same thing as investment readiness.

The composition of the syndicate matters just as much as its existence. In diaspora deals, the most effective groups often combine one investor with local market fluency, one with sector depth, and one with access to later-stage or international capital. That mix is more powerful than simply gathering many small cheques from the same community. It gives the founder clearer support and gives the syndicate a better chance of surviving the awkward moments that come after closing: missed milestones, bridge discussions, redomiciliation questions, or the arrival of a strong outside lead who wants the round cleaned up before investing. A syndicate should therefore be built around complementary competence, not social symmetry.

Syndication also changes behavior after the deal closes, which is one reason it deserves to be designed carefully at the outset. A founder supported by several investors may benefit from broader advice, but only if the group has a discipline for how support is given. Without that discipline, the founder receives conflicting requests and the lead investor becomes a traffic controller rather than a strategic partner. Good syndicates prevent this by clarifying who owns which part of the support role. One investor may lead commercial introductions, another may focus on governance, and another may help prepare later fundraising. In cross-border diaspora deals, that division can be the difference between helpful involvement and exhausting interference.

Lead selection is especially important where investors are split between diaspora members abroad and operating partners on the ground. A local investor may be better at verifying payments, contracts, and regulatory realities. An overseas lead may be better at syndicate management, later-stage investor communication, and institutional reporting expectations. Mature syndicates use both vantage points. They avoid the common mistake of assuming that one person can perform every function equally well just because that person sourced the deal.

3 When SPVs Help and When They Complicate the Transaction

Special-purpose vehicles, or SPVs, are often introduced as an administrative convenience. In one sense, they are. Instead of placing a large number of individual investors directly on the cap table, an SPV allows them to invest through a single entity. This can simplify documentation, voting arrangements, information flow, and later-round negotiations. For founders, that reduction in cap-table clutter is valuable. For investors, an SPV can concentrate governance in the hands of a lead or manager who has both the authority and the responsibility to speak for the group.

The attraction of the SPV is strongest when a round includes several diaspora investors writing relatively small tickets. Without an SPV, the company may face disproportionate legal and administrative costs for a modest amount of capital. With an SPV, the group can pool diligence, standardize subscription mechanics, and centralize reporting. Entrepreneurial-finance texts make this point clearly: the structure chosen at entry affects not only the cost of closing the round, but also the efficiency of follow-on investing, rights management, and exit execution (Alemany & Andreoli, 2026; Mustafa, 2021).

But an SPV is not a free simplification. It moves complexity from the company's cap table into the vehicle itself. Someone must manage onboarding, compliance, governance, reporting, and sometimes investor disagreement. If the SPV manager lacks authority, every decision becomes slow. If the manager has authority but weak accountability, minority investors may feel trapped inside a structure they do not really control. These are not theoretical risks. Cross-border early-stage deals already suffer from delayed information and interpretive gaps. A badly designed SPV can amplify both.

The best use cases are therefore fairly specific. An SPV works well when there is a credible lead investor, a shared investment thesis, a manageable number of participants, and a clear plan for how decisions will be taken on follow-on rounds, waivers, exits, and disputes. It is especially useful when future investors are likely to prefer a clean cap table and a single line of communication. It is less attractive when investors are highly heterogeneous, when the lead lacks the bandwidth to manage the vehicle, or when the underlying jurisdictional and tax issues are still poorly understood. In those cases, direct co-investment or a smaller, more tightly organized syndicate may be the better answer. In practice, the structure should fit the coordination problem rather than the fashion of the moment.

An SPV can also create hidden tax and regulatory questions if it is chosen too quickly. Investors may assume that pooling everyone into one entity will simplify life across the board, only to discover that onboarding, beneficial-ownership disclosure, withholding treatment, or reporting obligations become heavier inside the vehicle. The problem is rarely the concept of the SPV itself. The problem is using it before mapping the jurisdictions involved, the identity of likely future investors, and the real governance burden that the manager will carry. Good SPVs are operational solutions. Weak SPVs are administrative optimism with legal documents attached.

There are also situations in which direct investment remains the cleaner route. Family offices, experienced diaspora founders turned angels, or a small group of long-time co-investors may not need an SPV if they already share decision norms and can tolerate direct cap-table visibility. In those cases, adding a vehicle may simply add cost. The right question is not whether an SPV is modern or common. It is whether it solves a real coordination problem. When it does, it can materially improve the investability of the round. When it does not, it becomes one more layer founders must explain to the next investor.

There is a reputational dimension too. Founders remember whether an SPV helped create a professional investor interface or merely concentrated confusion inside a formal shell. Later-stage investors notice the same thing. A clean vehicle with disciplined reporting can make a seed round look institutionally stronger than its size would suggest. A badly administered one can make a promising company appear immature. In diaspora markets where trust and reputation travel quickly, that difference affects future pipeline quality as much as any one transaction.

4 Legal Basics that Change Deal Economics

In cross-border diaspora angel deals, legal terms are not secondary details added after valuation. They are part of valuation itself. In thin markets, where comparables are scarce, institutional signals are difficult to verify, and exits are uncertain, the headline pre-money price rarely tells the full economic story. Two deals with the same valuation may have very different risk-return profiles depending on information rights, enforceability, currency exposure, shareholder protections, liquidation preferences, transfer restrictions, syndicate coordination, and exit rights. For diaspora angels, the legal architecture of the deal is therefore not a technical appendix. It is one of the main ways uncertainty becomes investable.

This point is particularly important because diaspora angels often invest across different legal systems, currencies, governance norms, and enforcement environments. Their network familiarity can reduce informational opacity, but it cannot eliminate legal risk. Formal institutions and culture shape venture-capital activity across countries, while relational and institutional trust influence cross-border investment behavior (Hain et al., 2016; Li & Zahra, 2012). In practical terms, trust may help an investor identify a credible founder, but it does not automatically secure reporting discipline, protect against dilution, clarify ownership, or guarantee exit enforceability. The term sheet must therefore convert trust into rights, procedures, milestones, and decision rules.

The first task is to identify the legal blind spots that frequently distort cross-border angel deals. These blind spots are easy to underestimate because they often remain invisible at signing. They become costly later, when the company needs follow-on capital, when information quality deteriorates, when a founder issues new shares, when currency controls delay transfers, or when a strategic buyer requires cleaner governance before acquisition. Table 1 summarizes the legal issues that most often turn an apparently attractive valuation into a fragile investment structure.

The implication of Table 1 is that legal blind spots should not be treated as post-closing technicalities. They directly affect valuation because they determine whether investors can monitor performance, participate in future rounds, protect against dilution, manage currency exposure, prevent value leakage, and exit under realistic conditions. A diaspora angel who accepts a superficially attractive valuation while ignoring these issues may not have bought into a cheap deal. They may have accepted hidden risk that should have been priced, structured, or rejected.

The second task is to translate these blind spots into proportionate term-sheet responses. The right response depends on the source of uncertainty. Weak information quality requires reporting rights. Follow-on uncertainty requires staged financing and reserve planning. Exit uncertainty requires liquidation preferences, exit consultation rights, and a realistic exit map. Governance drift requires reserved matters or board observation. Syndicate fragmentation may require a syndicate SPV. ESG or climate claims require measurable covenants rather than narrative premiums.

This logic is especially relevant for diaspora angels because their investments often combine relational trust with formal uncertainty. The temptation is to rely on community endorsement, shared origin, founder reputation, or personal familiarity. Those signals are valuable, but they should not replace documentation. Diaspora investors are strongest when they use relational proximity to sharpen legal and commercial diligence, not when they allow proximity to soften discipline.

Table 2 should be read as a matching device rather than as a rigid template. Its purpose is to prevent investors from responding to all uncertainty through price alone. In thin markets, a blanket discount can be crude and sometimes damaging. If the problem is poor reporting, the answer is not necessarily a much lower valuation;

Table 1 Legal blind spots that frequently distort cross-border angel deals

Legal blind spot	How it distorts deal economics	Practical question for diaspora angels
Weak information rights	Investors cannot verify performance, cash use, contracts, or milestone progress	What reports, documents, and access rights are required after closing?
Unclear governing law and enforceability	Rights may be difficult to enforce across jurisdictions	Which law governs the agreement, and where can disputes be resolved?
Messy cap table	Follow-on investors may avoid the deal or demand restructuring	Is ownership clean, documented, and understandable to later investors?
Founder dilution or over-dilution	Excessive early dilution weakens founder incentives and future fundability	Does the ownership structure preserve founder motivation and future round viability?
Missing pro rata rights	Investors may be diluted in future rounds without protection	Can early investors maintain participation if the company progresses?
Undefined milestone triggers	Tranche release becomes disputed or subjective	Are milestones objective, observable, dated, and verifiable?
Currency and transfer restrictions	Returns may be eroded or trapped by FX movements or capital controls	In which currency are investments, reporting, and distributions defined?
Weak IP ownership	Strategic buyers or later investors may discount or reject the company	Does the company clearly own or control its core intellectual property?
Related-party transactions	Value can leak through founder-linked suppliers, family entities, or opaque contracts	Are related-party transactions disclosed and subject to consent?
ESG or impact claims without evidence	Climate, community, or development narratives may inflate valuation	Which ESG or impact indicators are material, measurable, and reportable?
Fragmented diaspora syndicate	Many small investors create governance noise and cap-table complexity	Is there a lead investor or SPV to coordinate the group?
Unclear exit rights	Investors may have no practical route to liquidity or sale participation	What rights apply in sale, drag-along, tag-along, or exit negotiations?

Source Author's own elaboration based on Kontakos and Stavrou (2025), Park (2021), Brinkerhoff (2012), and related sources cited in the chapter it may be stronger information rights. If the problem is uncertainty about product-market fit, the answer may be a smaller first ticket and a second tranche tied to commercial evidence. If the problem is syndicate fragmentation, the answer may be an SPV and a designated lead investor. If the problem is an unverified climate or impact claim, the answer may be a measurable KPI and reporting covenant rather than an impact premium.

Information rights are the most basic protection. They give investors the ability to distinguish temporary underperformance from structural weakness. Monthly management accounts, cash-flow reports, material contract updates, cap-table changes, and use-of-proceeds reporting can all change deal economics because they reduce the cost of monitoring. Without these rights, diaspora angels may rely too heavily on informal updates, which can become unreliable as the company grows or faces stress.

Staged tranches are equally important. Angel investing is characterized by uncertainty, incomplete contracting, and ongoing involvement (Edelman et al., 2017). In thin markets, this means that commitment timing matters as much as headline price. Mustafa (2021) shows that early-stage investing depends heavily on how

Table 2 From valuation problem to term-sheet response

Valuation problem	Term-sheet response	Practical discipline
Weak information quality	Information rights, monthly reporting, access to management accounts	Do not price on narrative alone
Follow-on uncertainty	Staged tranches, milestone-based release, investor reserve planning	Avoid overcommitting too early
Exit uncertainty	Liquidation preference, exit consultation rights, realistic exit map	Protect downside without suffocating the firm
Founder dilution risk	Smaller initial ticket, founder-friendly option pool, staged valuation adjustment	Avoid weakening future incentives
Governance drift	Reserved matters, board observer, consent rights for major decisions	Match control to actual risk
Currency or transfer risk	Local-currency provisions, FX adjustment logic, clear remittance terms	Avoid hidden valuation erosion
Syndicate fragmentation	Syndicate SPV, lead investor rights, pro rata rules, standardised reporting	Reduce coordination costs among diaspora angels
ESG or climate claim	ESG covenant, use-of-proceeds reporting, impact KPI	Prevent impact-washing and valuation inflation

Source Author's own elaboration

investors pace capital, preserve optionality, and support venture development. Milestone tranches should therefore be tied to objective and observable events: signed contracts, paid pilots, regulatory clearance, retained customers, gross-margin visibility, or export activation. Vague triggers such as "market traction" or "strategic progress" should be avoided because they create disputes rather than discipline.

Downside protection also requires proportionality. Thin markets do not justify predatory terms. They justify clear terms. Liquidation preferences, pro rata rights, reserved matters, and board observation can be appropriate when they address specific economic risks. But heavy control rights can damage founder trust, reduce agility, and make future rounds more difficult. The guiding principle should be proportionality: use the lightest contractual mechanism that addresses the relevant risk.

Syndicate SPVs deserve special attention in diaspora investing. Cross-border angel investment is often fragmented, with many small investors contributing modest tickets from different countries. Mason et al. (2022) show that cross-border angel investing faces constraints linked to information, networks, and institutional fragmentation. Wesemann and Antretter (2023) further suggest that larger syndicates can reduce sensitivity to geographic and cultural distance and improve returns. A syndicate SPV can simplify the cap table, designate one lead investor, standardize rights, coordinate tranche release, and represent the group in follow-on or exit negotiations. For founders, this can be valuable because it replaces a dispersed investor crowd with one organized counterparty.

Finally, ESG and climate-related claims should be treated with the same discipline as financial claims. A founder may present a venture as climate-enabling, community-oriented, or developmentally important. That may be true, but it should not automatically increase valuation. If ESG value is part of the investment case, it should be translated into material indicators, reporting obligations, and governance safeguards. Otherwise, impact language can become another form of overpricing.

The practical lesson is straightforward. In thin markets, good legal design does not replace trust. It makes trust investable. For diaspora angels, the best term sheets are not the most aggressive ones. They are the ones that convert uncertainty into observable evidence, proportionate rights, staged commitments, coordinated governance, and realistic exit options. That is how legal basics change deal economics, and how diaspora capital can cross borders without losing discipline.

5 A Practical Sequencing Model for Mature Cross-Border Deals

The literature points toward a sequencing principle that is more useful than any one template. First, decide who is leading. A serious cross-border round needs a party responsible for diligence coordination, document flow, negotiation discipline, and post-close oversight. Without that role, syndicates drift. Second, build the diligence stack in layers. Commercial logic comes first, then legal and tax feasibility, then instrument choice. Founders and investors often reverse this order by debating structure before they know whether the opportunity is truly investable.

Third, select the structure that solves the actual coordination problem. If one experienced investor is writing the bulk of the cheque and a small number of co-investors will add sector knowledge, direct co-investment may be sufficient. If many smaller diaspora investors wish to participate and future rounds will matter, an SPV may be justified. If the key benefit comes from pooling diligence and post-investment support rather than cap-table simplification, a lead-led syndicate can work without an SPV. Mason et al. (2022) and Harrison (2022) both suggest that better cross-border angel investing depends as much on architecture and support mechanisms as on investor enthusiasm.

Fourth, translate trust into explicit rights. Information rights, reserved matters, board or observer roles, pro rata rights, transfer restrictions, and exit mechanics should be chosen deliberately. Over-documenting everything can cripple a young company, but under-documenting recurring flashpoints simply postpones conflict. The right balance is contextual. A founder operating in a market with weak disclosure norms may need stronger reporting covenants. An investor group that expects follow-on participation may care most about pro rata rights and cap-table hygiene. A deal exposed to heavy regulatory risk may need clearer escalation and consent mechanics around major operational decisions.

Finally, plan for strain before it appears. How will investors decide on bridge finance? What happens if one investor wants to exit early? Who speaks to a later-stage lead? What happens if the company needs to redomicile, clean up intellectual-property ownership, or open a foreign holding structure for a strategic partnership? Cross-border deals rarely fail because nobody liked the opportunity. They fail because structure lagged behind ambition. Mature diaspora angel investing avoids that trap by treating syndicates, SPVs, and legal basics as part of investment performance rather than back-office detail.

Post-close governance should be planned with the same seriousness as closing mechanics. A cross-border deal with diaspora investors benefits from a reporting calendar that is predictable and light enough to sustain. Monthly cash and runway reporting, quarterly operating updates, a clear process for approving material deviations, and an agreed protocol for emergency decisions can prevent mistrust from building around simple communication delays. Many young companies do not fail because the business case was false. They fail because uncertainty was allowed to accumulate without a routine for turning information into shared judgment. Mature structuring anticipates that problem from day one.

Later-stage investors also tend to reward structural cleanliness. A seed or angel round that was tolerable when the company was tiny can become a deterrent when a larger investor arrives and sees fragmented rights, unclear voting blocks, or unresolved ownership questions. Founders often experience this as an unpleasant surprise. Investors should not. One of the quiet strengths of disciplined early structuring is that it preserves option value for later capital. The round is easier to diligence, easier to model, and easier to negotiate when governance was coherent from the start. In

Table 3 Structuring options for cross-border diaspora angel deals

Structure	Best use case	Main strength	Main watch-out
Single lead investor with co-investors	Small round with clear leadership	Fast decisions and direct accountability	Too much dependence on one investor's capacity
Lead-led syndicate	Cross-border deal needing pooled diligence and follow-on support	Blends sector, local, and network knowledge	Can become slow if decision rights are vague
SPV	Many smaller investors and a need for cap-table simplicity	One line on the cap table and centralized governance	Complexity moves into the vehicle and must be managed
Direct scattered investors	Rarely ideal in thin cross-border deals	Low setup burden at the start	Administrative load, weak coordination, and messy future rounds
Parallel local and foreign entities with a clear holding logic	Operating business spans more than one jurisdiction	Separates local operations from investor-facing ownership	Can create confusion if ownership mapping is weak
Informal club-style investor group	Rarely suitable beyond very small experimental rounds	Low setup cost at the start	Weak governance and difficult follow-on positioning

Source Author's own elaboration based on Paul and Whittam (2010), Mason et al. (2022), Harrison (2022), Mustafa (2021), and Alemany and Andreoli (2026)

thin markets, where good later-stage investors may already be scarce, this matters more than founders initially realize.

The practical discipline here is sequencing with friction in mind. Ask first what later investors, acquirers, or institutional partners will want to see when they look back at the angel round. If the answer includes clean ownership, clear authority, manageable investor lines, and documented rights, then those elements should be built in at entry. Cross-border diaspora deals are at their best when they feel socially grounded but institutionally legible to people who were never part of the original relationship chain. Table 3 summarizes the structuring options that connect those frictions with workable investment vehicles.

6 Conclusion

Valuation in thin markets is best understood as a governance problem with financial consequences. The issue is not whether an investor can produce a valuation number, but whether that number remains defensible once weak comparables, institutional friction, signal distortion, currency exposure, fragmented syndicates, legal blind spots, and uncertain exits are made explicit. In such contexts, valuation is not a single calculation. It is a disciplined process through which investors decide which risks should affect price, which should be managed through structure, and which should prevent the deal from proceeding.

Diaspora angels hold a distinctive advantage because they can reduce opacity through language, familiarity, local knowledge, and networked trust. They may understand founder reputation, market access, payment behavior, regulatory bottlenecks, and informal verification channels better than ordinary foreign investors. Yet this advantage must sharpen diligence rather than inflate valuation. Homeland affinity, community pride, or emotional attachment can widen the set of opportunities worth examining, but they should never replace commercial evidence, legal discipline, or exit realism.

The first recommendation for diaspora angels is to disaggregate uncertainty before discussing price. Venture risk, context risk, execution risk, governance risk, currency risk, ESG risk, and exit risk should not be collapsed into a single country discount. Weak information quality should be addressed through reporting rights and access to management accounts. Follow-on uncertainty should be managed through smaller initial tickets, reserve planning, and milestone-based tranches. Governance drift should be handled through proportionate reserved matters or board observation. Currency and transfer risk require explicit provisions. ESG or climate claims should be tied to measurable indicators and reporting obligations.

The second recommendation is to treat the term sheet as part of valuation. A superficially attractive price may conceal weak enforceability, messy ownership, unclear IP rights, missing pro rata rights, undefined milestone triggers, or fragmented investor coordination. Conversely, a fair valuation supported by information rights, staged capital, founder-friendly dilution, syndicate coordination, and realistic downside protection may create a stronger investment structure. In thin markets, legal design does not replace trust; it makes trust investable.

The third recommendation is to use syndication deliberately. Diaspora investors often contribute small tickets across geographies. Without coordination, this can create cap-table complexity and weak monitoring. A syndicate SPV can pool capital, designate a lead investor, standardize reporting, coordinate tranche release, and represent investors in follow-on or exit discussions. For founders, this also improves future fundability by replacing fragmented diaspora capital with a more legible investor structure.

The fourth recommendation is to begin with the exit map. Entry valuation should reflect plausible buyers, governance thresholds, time-to-exit, and the likelihood of later-stage capital, not imported multiples from deeper ecosystems. Investors should identify realistic local, regional, and cross-border exit routes before pricing the deal.

Ultimately, disciplined valuation is also ecosystem building. When diaspora angels price on evidence rather than excitement, structure uncertainty rather than ignore it, and support founders with credible milestones and clean governance, they create better reference points for future deals. Diaspora capital generates local impact not by suspending financial discipline, but by combining trust, structure, and realism in markets where all three are scarce.

References

Alemany, L., & Andreoli, J. J. (Eds.). (2026). *Entrepreneurial finance: The art and science of growing ventures* (2nd ed.). Cambridge University Press. https://doi.org/10.1017/9781009537827

Brinkerhoff, J. M. (2012). Creating an enabling environment for diasporas' participation in homeland development. *International Migration, 50*(1), 75–95. https://doi.org/10.1111/j.1468-2435.2009.00542.x

Edelman, L. F., Manolova, T. S., & Brush, C. G. (2017). Angel investing: A literature review. *Foundations and Trends in Entrepreneurship, 13*(4–5), 265–439. https://doi.org/10.1561/0300000051

Hain, D., Johan, S. A., & Wang, D. (2016). Determinants of cross-border venture capital investments in emerging and developed economies: The effects of relational and institutional trust. *Journal of Business Ethics, 138*(4), 743–764. https://doi.org/10.1007/s10551-015-2772-4

Harrison, R. T. (2022). "Pennies from heaven"? Market failure, circuits of capital and policy support for business angels: The case of cross-border angel investment. *Journal of Business Venturing Insights, 17*, Article e00311. https://doi.org/10.1016/j.jbvi.2022.e00311

Kontakos, P., & Stavrou, S. (2025). Israeli and Jewish diaspora investment in Cyprus: FDI determinants, entry modes, and institutional challenges. *Journal of East-West Business*. Advance online publication. https://doi.org/10.1080/10669868.2025.2595351

Lerner, J., Schoar, A., Sokolinski, S., & Wilson, K. (2018). The globalization of angel investments: Evidence across countries. *Journal of Financial Economics, 127*(1), 1–20. https://doi.org/10.1016/j.jfineco.2017.05.012

Li, Y., & Zahra, S. A. (2012). Formal institutions, culture, and venture capital activity: A cross-country analysis. *Journal of Business Venturing, 27*(1), 95–111. https://doi.org/10.1016/j.jbusvent.2010.06.003

Mason, C., Botelho, T., & Duggett, J. (2022). Promoting cross-border investing by business angels in the European Union. *Regional Studies, 56*(8), 1391–1403. https://doi.org/10.1080/00343404.2021.1960961

Mestwerdt, S., Mrożewski, M., Sydow, A., & Burkert, N. (2025). Unveiling signaling processes in early-stage cross-border investment: Evidence from South African entrepreneurs and European business angels. *Journal of World Business, 60*(5), Article 101662. https://doi.org/10.1016/j.jwb.2025.101662

Mustafa, M. (2021). *Angel investing: The untold story of India*. Palgrave Macmillan. https://doi.org/10.1007/978-981-16-0921-3

Park, S. B. (2021). Courting foreign direct investment from diasporas: Are diaspora engagement policies effective? Under what conditions? *Pacific Focus, 36*(2), 252–286. https://doi.org/10.1111/pafo.12188

Paul, S., & Whittam, G. (2010). Business angel syndicates: An exploratory study of gatekeepers. *Venture Capital, 12*(3), 241–256. https://doi.org/10.1080/13691061003711438

Wesemann, H., & Antretter, T. (2023). The internationalization of business angel networks: Do syndicates increase cross-border investment returns? *Venture Capital, 25*(4), 487–514. https://doi.org/10.1080/13691066.2022.2082898

Climate-Linked Diaspora Bonds and Blended Impact Vehicles: Conditions for Credible Mobilization

Nadia Zahoor, Muhammad Saleem Sumbal, Marc Poulin, Divya Upadhyay, and Eiman Ashraf

Abstract This chapter examines when climate-linked diaspora bonds and related impact vehicles can mobilize capital credibly and when they are likely to disappoint. It does not advocate a new instrument. Instead, it synthesizes evidence from diaspora-finance, remittance, sovereign-bond, blue-finance, and business-angel research to clarify the operating conditions under which diaspora capital can support climate mitigation, resilience, and adaptation. The chapter shows that homeland attachment can widen investor attention, but sustained uptake depends on governance quality, ring-fenced use of proceeds, investable project pipelines, and credible intermediation. It also explains why remittances, although large and resilient, do not automatically become productive investment without financial-sector depth. By comparing sovereign diaspora bonds, thematic climate notes, and blended vehicles, the chapter develops an evidence-based framework for choosing the right instrument for the right problem. The central conclusion is clear: climate-linked diaspora finance works best when treated as serious financial architecture rather than patriotic fundraising.

N. Zahoor (✉)
School of Business and Management, Queen Mary University of London, London, UK
e-mail: n.zahoor@qmul.ac.uk

Innolab, University of Vaasa, Vaasa, Finland

Department of Management and Marketing, King Fahd University of Petroleum and Minerals, Dhahran, Saudi Arabia

M. S. Sumbal
Department of Industrial and Systems Engineering, The Hong Kong Polytechnic University, Hong Kong, China

M. Poulin · D. Upadhyay
Entrepreneurship & Innovation Centre, Abu Dhabi School of Management, Abu Dhabi, United Arab Emirates
e-mail: m.poulin@adsm.ac.ae

D. Upadhyay
e-mail: d.upadhyay@adsm.ac.ae

E. Ashraf
City University Ajman, Ajman, United Arab Emirates

H. Jarrar et al. (eds.), *Diaspora Angel Investing*, Ethnic and Indigenous Business Studies, https://doi.org/10.1007/978-3-032-33088-8_6

1 Introduction

Climate adaptation, energy transition, and resilience financing all face a familiar problem: the need for patient capital is large, while trusted long-term funding channels remain thin in many lower- and middle-income economies. Diaspora capital is often presented as a partial answer. The idea is intuitively attractive. Migrants and diaspora communities retain emotional ties to their countries of origin, often hold foreign currency savings, and may be willing to finance public-purpose investment that conventional markets underprice. Yet the evidence is less romantic than the rhetoric. Diaspora finance can matter, but it only becomes durable when the instrument is credible, the use of proceeds is clear, and the intermediating institutions are trusted (Asiedu et al., 2024; Nanziri et al., 2025).

The scale of the underlying resource is undeniable. Officially recorded remittances to low- and middle-income countries were expected to reach $685 billion in 2024, a level larger than foreign direct investment and official development assistance combined, with India alone estimated at $129 billion (Ratha et al., 2024). Even so, remittances and diaspora investment are not interchangeable. Household transfers are designed for income support, consumption smoothing, education, housing, and informal insurance. Climate-linked investment vehicles require very different conditions: longer tenors, clearer reporting, more formal governance, and stronger mechanisms for pooling and deploying capital.

Diaspora finance also needs to be understood alongside the wider entrepreneurship and immigrant enterprise literature, which shows that migrant economic behavior is rarely reducible to simple financial calculation. Migrant and immigrant entrepreneurs mobilize multiple forms of capital across home and host contexts, including financial, social, cultural, symbolic, and institutional resources (Yasin & Poulin, 2025; Yasin et al., 2025a, 2025b, 2026a). This matters for climate-linked diaspora instruments because homeland attachment may generate initial attention, but the conversion of attachment into investable commitment depends on trust, legitimacy, and the perceived credibility of the institutional channel through which capital is mobilized.

This chapter asks a narrower and more practical question than the usual "Can diaspora finance help?" It asks under what conditions climate-linked diaspora bonds and related impact vehicles become credible enough to attract capital repeatedly. The answer, as the literature shows, depends less on patriotic messaging than on design discipline. Climate labels can help. They also raise the standard of proof.

That need for credibility is even more acute in climate finance than in ordinary homeland investing because the maturity profile is longer and the political visibility is higher. Climate-linked projects often require years before their economic and environmental value is fully visible. Investors therefore lend or commit capital against governance, implementation discipline, and reporting quality long before the final outcome can be observed. Diaspora finance can help fill this gap, but only if it enters through structures capable of surviving long holding periods and repeated scrutiny. Climate urgency does not relax financial architecture. It makes it more important.

2 What Diaspora Bonds Do Well—And What They Do Not

Diaspora bonds are most convincing when they solve a funding problem that investors can recognize and when the issuer already possesses enough credibility to borrow at scale. Their advantage is not that diaspora investors ignore risk. It is that some investors may accept a narrower risk premium when they understand the country, identify with the national purpose, or value participation beyond pure yield. Gillespie et al. (1999) captured this logic early by showing that homeland investment interest has both economic and identity-based components. Park and Tuxhorn (2025) sharpen the point with newer evidence: emotional and social drivers complement financial logic, but do not replace it. That finding should anchor any mature discussion of diaspora bonds.

The experience of successful issuers makes the same point in institutional form. Schneidman et al. (2022) and Gevorkyan (2021) both note that, despite the appeal of diaspora bonds, only India and Israel have managed repeated large-scale success. That fact matters because it shows what success has depended on historically: long-standing market access, strong distribution networks, credible state capacity, and diasporas with a preexisting willingness to hold homeland-related instruments. Diaspora bonds did not succeed in those cases because patriotism overruled finance. They succeeded because patriotism was layered onto investable infrastructure. This point is consistent with research on immigrant entrepreneurship, which shows that transnational economic participation is shaped by the interaction between opportunity structures, resource access, and identity-based legitimacy rather than by ethnicity or belonging alone (Yasin, 2022; Yasin et al., 2025a, 2025b). Yasin and colleagues' work on immigrant enterprise in the UK, UAE, and other non-traditional entrepreneurship settings further suggests that financial capital is unevenly accessed and socially mediated, making credibility and intermediation central to whether migrant-linked resources become productive enterprise investment (Yasin et al., 2025a, 2025b, 2026b). This reinforces the chapter's argument that diaspora bonds cannot rely on patriotic affiliation as a substitute for disciplined financial design.

This is why unsuccessful or underused diaspora bond attempts often disappoint for predictable reasons. Governments assume that diaspora belonging automatically creates demand, then offer vague use-of-proceeds language, weak reporting, and no convincing answer on how the instrument fits broader debt management. Investors, especially professionals inside the diaspora, read those gaps quickly. They are often more, not less, sensitive to governance weaknesses because they combine familiarity with an external benchmark for what disciplined issuance looks like. Emotional proximity can therefore heighten scrutiny rather than soften it.

A useful implication follows. Diaspora bonds are strongest when they are framed as one instrument within a broader public-finance strategy, not as a substitute for credibility. They can widen the investor base, diversify funding, and support national projects with symbolic and economic salience. They cannot compensate for weak governance, unclear debt strategy, or an absence of investable assets. In practice, they work when the issuer is already serious enough to be trusted without them.

Seen properly, a diaspora bond is not a substitute for project selection or implementation discipline. It is a distribution and funding channel. The real economic work still depends on what sits behind the instrument: the sovereign balance sheet, the implementing agency, the project pipeline, and the reporting system. This distinction is easy to miss because bond discussions often focus on marketing to diaspora communities. Yet for climate-linked issuance the central question is whether the underlying assets or programs are financeable and monitorable. If they are not, diaspora distribution simply broadens attention to a weak proposition.

Investor heterogeneity needs to be kept in view. Some diaspora participants approach homeland instruments as conservative savers. Others are mission-oriented professionals willing to take measured thematic exposure. Others still are entrepreneurs or business owners who are used to higher-risk opportunities. Treating this spectrum as one audience is one reason diaspora bond initiatives become blunt. Climate-linked products should be designed for the investor base they actually target. Serious capital mobilization depends on matching disclosure, ticket size, tenor, and liquidity expectations to that investor segment rather than assuming that identity alone creates homogenous demand.

A mature issuer therefore begins with investor mapping rather than generic outreach. Which part of the diaspora is being approached? Are these buyers accustomed to sovereign paper, thematic products, venture risk, or savings instruments? The answer changes distribution strategy and product design. It also changes how the climate story should be told. Professional diaspora investors may need portfolio logic and risk treatment. Retail diaspora buyers may need clarity on safety, use of proceeds, and liquidity. The same climate message cannot carry the full burden across all these audiences.

3 Why Climate Linkage Raises the Bar

Adding a climate label changes the proposition. It can broaden appeal among diaspora investors who want measurable environmental and developmental impact. It can also align the instrument with urgent investment needs in power systems, water, transport resilience, coastal protection, and low-carbon urban infrastructure. Yet climate linkage raises the standard in three ways. First, investors expect a more explicit theory of use of proceeds. Second, they expect impact reporting that is periodic and intelligible. Third, they assume the underlying project pipeline is sufficiently developed to absorb capital without drift. Without these features, the climate label quickly begins to look cosmetic.

Research on sovereign green and thematic bonds underscores that point. Owusu-Mante et al. (2025) show that the effectiveness of sovereign green bonds in emerging economies depends on how they are integrated into broader policy frameworks and reporting systems. Romagnoli and Santini (2025) add that sovereign climate risk and bond-market dynamics are closely intertwined, making credibility around exposure and scarcity effects important for investors. In other words, climate-labeled debt is not just conventional debt with better language. It depends on the quality of the framework around it.

Lessons from blue finance and ring-fenced thematic instruments point in the same direction. Benzaken et al. (2024) show, in the Seychelles case, that moving from concept to practice required institutional coordination, implementation capacity, and a structure that investors could actually understand. Rogge (2025) makes a related point in the blue-bond literature by emphasizing that sustainable thematic finance succeeds when the instrument is linked to a clear policy and asset pipeline rather than a generic sustainability narrative. For diaspora investors, this discipline may matter even more because climate and homeland sentiment can create inflated expectations if disclosure is weak.

There is also a useful bridge to the early-stage impact-investing literature. Viglialoro et al. (2025) show that social-impact business angels differ from conventional angels not because they ignore economics, but because they integrate impact concerns explicitly into screening and portfolio management. Botelho et al. (2023) find similar nuance in green angel investing: motivations vary, yet serious investors still evaluate commercial viability carefully. Climate-linked diaspora instruments should be understood in the same way. Impact orientation may expand investor interest, but only when measurement, governance, and expected financial performance are treated with discipline. Climate linkage does not lower the threshold for credibility. It raises it. The credibility challenge is especially important in emerging-economy and Gulf contexts, where entrepreneurship and sustainability agendas are often intertwined with national development strategies, institutional modernization, and policy signaling. Recent work on entrepreneurship education, university-industry collaboration, and enterprise ecosystems in the UAE and wider MENA region shows that policy ambition only becomes durable when it is supported by institutional capacity, clear governance, and credible implementation mechanisms (Yasin & Gilani, 2022; Yasin & Khansari, 2021; Yasin & Nabi, 2026; Yasin et al., 2023). The same principle applies to climate-linked diaspora finance: aspirational framing can open political and investor attention, but credibility depends on whether institutional arrangements can withstand scrutiny.

For that reason, climate-linked diaspora instruments benefit from the disciplines already used in strong thematic debt markets: a published framework, a credible definition of eligible assets, external review where feasible, and regular reporting on both allocation and outcomes. Investors do not expect perfect impact measurement from the first issuance. They do expect a clear chain from subscription to deployment. Where that chain is weak, climate language can backfire because it raises expectations that the issuer is not prepared to meet. In diaspora settings the reputational damage may be larger because investors are discussing the instrument within communities that retain memory over time.

Climate additionality also matters. A climate-linked diaspora bond should not merely relabel expenditures that would have been funded anyway unless the issuer is prepared to say so transparently and explain the strategic rationale. Investors increasingly distinguish between labeled finance that changes capital allocation and labeled finance that merely changes presentation. That distinction is important for diaspora investors because many of them already give, remit, or invest informally in climate-relevant activities at home. A formal vehicle must therefore show why it offers something better: stronger scale, clearer accountability, or more disciplined deployment than informal support can achieve.

Measurement should also be proportionate. Investors need enough information to judge whether proceeds are being used as promised and whether the climate claim has substance. They do not need an impossible level of precision on day one. The most credible frameworks are often those that are concrete, limited, and consistent rather than encyclopedic. A smaller set of defensible metrics—such as energy saved, emissions avoided, water secured, or resilience assets delivered—can do more for trust than a crowded dashboard no one believes. There is also a sustainability logic here. Studies on green strategic intent, artificial intelligence capability, circular economy goals, natural capital productivity, and renewable-energy feasibility suggest that climate and sustainability transitions depend not only on ambition, but on the organizational and technical capabilities required to translate intent into measurable outcomes (Luqman et al., 2023; Ul-Durar et al., 2025; Zahoor et al., 2025). For climate-linked diaspora instruments, this implies that reporting cannot be treated as a post-issuance communication exercise. It is part of the instrument's credibility architecture.

4 From Remittances to Investment: The Missing Intermediation Layer

One of the most persistent mistakes in policy debate is to assume that large remittance flows can be converted directly into climate investment with the right amount of national encouragement. The evidence says otherwise. Remittances are large, resilient, and socially important, but they do not automatically become formal entrepreneurial or infrastructure finance. Alhassan et al. (2025) show this clearly: remittances on their own do not produce a robust positive effect on formal business creation, whereas the relationship becomes more favorable when financial development is stronger. Giuliano and Ruiz-Arranz (2009) and Sobiech (2019) reach related conclusions from a macro-finance angle. Financial depth changes what remittance money can do. This also aligns with immigrant entrepreneurship research showing that access to financial capital is not evenly distributed across migrant groups and is often shaped by perceived legitimacy, embeddedness, and institutional trust (Yasin et al., 2025a, 2025b, 2026b). In cross-national contexts, some immigrant entrepreneurs are able to activate ethnic, family, and community resources, while others face exclusion from formal financial systems and must rely on informal or relational channels. The implication for diaspora climate finance is clear: remittance scale is not enough. The decisive issue is whether financial systems can convert dispersed household flows and homeland-oriented savings into governed, investable, and accountable vehicles.

That finding matters for climate-linked diaspora vehicles because the financing chain is longer and more demanding than in ordinary household transfer. Someone must pool savings, assess projects, manage currency risk, report on impact, and protect investor rights. In other words, the crucial variable is intermediation. Kakhkharov (2019) and Vaaler (2013) both suggest that diaspora-linked financial flows become more economically productive when formal institutions and investment channels can absorb them. Asiedu et al. (2024) make the broader development point: migrant resource flows matter, but their effect depends on how they are embedded in domestic financial and policy systems.

This is why climate-linked diaspora instruments often work better when they are connected to regulated intermediaries, development banks, professionally managed funds, or blended structures with clear loss-allocation rules. A sovereign diaspora bond can be appropriate for national resilience programs where debt management is strong and project pipelines are public. A smaller thematic note may fit ring-fenced portfolios with transparent revenue or budget support. A blended vehicle can make more sense when the target assets are too small, too heterogeneous, or too early-stage for straight sovereign issuance. The choice should follow the intermediation challenge, not the branding opportunity.

Once this is understood, the line between diaspora bonds and broader impact vehicles becomes clearer. The question is no longer whether diaspora communities care about climate resilience. Many do. The question is whether there is an institutional machine capable of transforming that interest into repeatable deployment. Without that machine, the money stays in remittance channels or in low-engagement savings products. With it, climate-linked diaspora finance becomes possible—but only because intermediation has made the risk legible.

Ticket size and investor segmentation are also practical design questions. A climate-linked diaspora vehicle aimed at affluent professional investors abroad can carry a different disclosure burden, tenor, and minimum subscription than a product aimed at smaller retail diaspora participants. Mixing these audiences without clarity is risky. Professional investors will demand institutional discipline. Smaller investors may need simpler products, trusted distribution, and clearer liquidity expectations. The best designs acknowledge these differences openly instead of assuming that all diaspora investors can be reached through one instrument with one narrative.

Project preparation capacity is another part of the missing middle. Even when investor appetite exists, climate projects often stall because feasibility work, permitting, aggregation, and contracting are underdeveloped. Financial intermediation alone cannot fix that. It needs to be paired with preparation capability. This is one reason blended vehicles or public-development partnerships often outperform standalone diaspora products in difficult settings. They do not just absorb risk. They help create investable assets. Without that preparation layer, climate-linked diaspora finance risks chasing pipelines that are politically compelling but financially premature.

Table 1 What prior experience suggests about climate-linked diaspora issuance

Experience base	What worked	What limited uptake	Design implication
Repeated diaspora bond programs	Distribution credibility and institutional continuity	Success proved hard to replicate elsewhere	Do not treat patriotism as a substitute for trust
Emerging-economy sovereign green bonds	Clear frameworks and reporting improved legitimacy	Weak integration with policy and pipeline reduced impact	Climate linkage must be operational, not decorative
Blue-finance and ring-fenced thematic vehicles	Defined asset use improved investor clarity	Complex governance raised execution demands	Ring-fencing helps only if implementation capacity exists
Remittance-rich but shallow financial systems	Large household flows created potential investor awareness	Weak intermediation blocked productive deployment	Build channels before launching products
Impact-led angel or diaspora venture vehicles	Closer investor engagement and mission alignment	Limited scale and uneven measurement practice	Use only where governance capacity matches ambition
Weakly defined climate labeling	Can attract initial attention	Creates skepticism and reputational risk	Naming must follow substance, not precede it

Local financial institutions can either accelerate or block this transition from remittance scale to climate investment. Where banks, development agencies, or capital-market intermediaries can warehouse projects, verify documentation, and handle investor servicing, diaspora products become far more plausible. Where those functions are missing, even a well-branded instrument struggles. This is why policy discussions that focus only on issuance mechanics often disappoint. The investability problem is not just on the investor side. It also sits in the domestic machinery that must receive and allocate capital responsibly. Table 1 synthesizes prior experience on climate-linked diaspora issuance and the design lessons that follow from it.

Source Author's own elaboration based on Schneidman et al. (2022), Gevorkyan (2021), Owusu-Mante et al. (2025), Benzaken et al. (2024), and Alhassan et al. (2025)

5 Choosing the Right Vehicle for the Right Problem

No single diaspora-climate instrument fits every financing gap. A sovereign diaspora bond is best suited to governments or public agencies that already possess credible debt-management systems, a transparent climate or resilience framework, and a pipeline large enough to justify issuance costs. Its strengths are scale, visibility, and the possibility of linking diaspora participation to national transition goals. Its weakness is equally obvious: if governance is weak or reporting vague, investor disappointment can damage future issuance beyond the climate theme itself.

A ring-fenced thematic note or project-linked vehicle works better when the purpose is narrower and more traceable. Water infrastructure, grid upgrades, coastal resilience, or municipal adaptation programs may lend themselves to this form if cash flows, implementing agencies, and monitoring arrangements are identifiable. The investor does not need perfection. The investor needs credible boundaries around what the instrument will and will not fund. Blue-finance experience shows that such boundaries can materially improve credibility when combined with external partners and disciplined reporting (Benzaken et al., 2024; Rogge, 2025).

Blended vehicles sit somewhere else on the spectrum. They are attractive when the goal is to finance pipelines that are too fragmented for sovereign issuance but too risky or illiquid for plain-vanilla diaspora subscription. In that setting, diaspora capital may play a catalytic role alongside development institutions, local banks, philanthropic capital, or first-loss mechanisms. The strength of the blended model is flexibility. Its weakness is complexity. If governance, valuation, currency treatment, and impact measurement are not explicit, the vehicle quickly becomes difficult to understand and therefore difficult to scale.

The central design lesson is therefore restraint. Use the simplest structure capable of matching investor expectations with project reality. Name the use of proceeds clearly. Build reporting that can survive scrutiny. Give investors an intelligible governance map. When climate-linked diaspora finance works, it does not do so because the instrument sounds inspiring. It works because the instrument is specific enough to be believed. This restrained design logic mirrors wider entrepreneurship research in the UAE and MENA region, where entrepreneurial ecosystems, incubators, and university-industry collaborations often succeed or fail according to the fit between institutional ambition and operational capability (Yasin & Gilani, 2022; Yasin & Khansari, 2021; Yasin & Nabi, 2026; Yasin et al., 2023). Climate-linked diaspora instruments should therefore avoid over-engineering. The more complex the vehicle, the greater the burden of explanation, governance, and investor protection. Simpler structures with clearer accountability may be more credible than ambitious blended vehicles whose risk allocation, climate additionality, or reporting logic is difficult to understand.

Foreign-exchange risk and liquidity also deserve explicit treatment. Climate and resilience assets are often domestic-currency uses of capital, while diaspora investors may subscribe in hard currency and benchmark their returns accordingly. If the currency problem is ignored, reported impact may look strong while real investor outcomes disappoint. Likewise, illiquidity is not necessarily fatal, but it must be named honestly. Investors can accept longer holding periods when they understand the trade-off and believe the reporting. They are far less patient when the instrument was presented as simple, liquid, and patriotic but behaves as complex, illiquid, and opaque.

Governance mechanisms should be visible enough to reassure investors but simple enough to operate. This may involve independent verification of allocation reports, advisory oversight for thematic integrity, explicit rules on refinancing or reallocation, and published triggers for material changes in the use of proceeds. None of these devices guarantees success. What they do is reduce ambiguity. In climate-linked diaspora finance ambiguity is costly because investors are evaluating both financial stewardship and mission fidelity. The clearer those responsibilities are, the more likely the instrument is to build repeat rather than one-off participation.

Distribution credibility is part of governance as well. Investors are more likely to accept a longer-tenor climate-linked diaspora product when it is offered through channels that already carry financial trust, whether that means recognized banks, public debt offices, regulated funds, or reputable development partners. The distribution channel signals seriousness before the first impact report is published. In markets where diaspora investors have seen one-off patriotic products come and go, this signal can be decisive. Table 2 compares the main climate-linked diaspora instruments and their operating conditions.

Table 2 Climate-linked diaspora instruments and their operating conditions

Instrument	Best fit	Main advantage	Main constraint
Sovereign diaspora bond	Large national resilience or energy-transition programs	Scale and national visibility	Requires strong sovereign credibility and reporting discipline
Ring-fenced thematic climate note	Defined adaptation or mitigation pipeline	Clearer use of proceeds and easier monitoring	Needs a mature project pipeline and governance clarity
Blended diaspora impact vehicle	Fragmented SME, clean-tech, or local infrastructure portfolios	Can absorb higher-risk assets through layered capital	Harder to govern, explain, and replicate
Traditional remittance channel	Household support and small-scale private use	Large, resilient flow base	Not designed for long-tenor climate investment without intermediation
Diaspora clean-tech or resilience fund/SPV	Smaller innovative ventures and fragmented project pipelines	Flexible deployment and thematic focus	Needs strong manager credibility and valuation discipline
Municipal or sub-sovereign resilience vehicle	Defined urban or regional adaptation pipeline	Closer link between financing and visible assets	Governance and disclosure demands can be heavy

Source Author's own elaboration based on Nanziri et al. (2025), Alhassan et al. (2025), Benzaken et al. (2024), Owusu-Mante et al. (2025), and related sources cited in the chapter

6 Conclusion

Climate-linked diaspora finance deserves neither dismissal nor romanticism. The literature points to a more disciplined middle position. Diaspora investors can widen the capital base for climate and resilience finance, especially where homeland ties, foreign-currency savings, and developmental motivation intersect. Yet the same literature is equally clear that this capital does not become investable simply because it is emotionally proximate. Credibility, disclosure, project readiness, and intermediation do the real work.

The practical conclusion is therefore straightforward. Countries and institutions should choose instruments that match their actual governance and pipeline capacity. Where sovereign credibility and climate frameworks are strong, diaspora bonds may be viable. Where projects are ring-fenced and measurable, thematic notes can work. Where assets are fragmented and risk is higher, blended vehicles are more realistic. In every case, climate-linked diaspora finance becomes durable only when the architecture is strong enough to be trusted repeatedly.

The chapter's argument also connects to a broader body of work on immigrant entrepreneurship and capital mobilization. Yasin and colleagues show that migrant enterprise is shaped by the interaction of capital access, embeddedness, legitimacy, and institutional context across different national settings (Yasin, 2022; Yasin & Hafeez, 2023; Yasin & Poulin, 2025; Yasin et al., 2025a, 2025b, 2026a, 2026b). Climate-linked diaspora finance can therefore be read as one extension of this wider problem: how mobile communities convert identity, trust, savings, and cross-border attachment into credible economic participation. Its success depends not on diaspora sentiment alone, but on whether that sentiment is matched with investable structures, serious governance, and a credible pathway from capital mobilization to developmental and climate outcomes.

The broader developmental point follows naturally. Countries do not need to prove that diaspora communities care about climate resilience; that concern is already visible in remittance behavior, philanthropy, and investment interest. What they need to prove is that climate-linked vehicles deserve to sit alongside those flows as formal, repeatable, investable options. Where that proof exists, diaspora finance can be catalytic. Where it does not, climate branding will remain louder than capital mobilization.

References

Alhassan, U., Maswana, J.-C., & Inaba, K. (2025). Leveraging remittances for entrepreneurship: The role of financial development in developing economies. *Journal of the Knowledge Economy*. Advance online publication. https://doi.org/10.1007/s13132-025-02819-1

Asiedu, E., Tapsoba, T. A., & Gelb, S. (2024). Migrant resource flows and development in the Global South. In H. Crawley & J. K. Teye (Eds.), *The Palgrave handbook of South–South migration and inequality* (pp. 519–542). Palgrave Macmillan. https://doi.org/10.1007/978-3-031-39814-8_24

Benzaken, D., Adam, J. P., Virdin, J., & Voyer, M. (2024). From concept to practice: Financing sustainable blue economy in Small Island Developing States, lessons learnt from the Seychelles experience. *Marine Policy, 163*, Article 106072. https://doi.org/10.1016/j.marpol.2024.106072

Botelho, T., Mason, C., & Chalvatzis, K. (2023). 50 shades of green—Angel investing in green businesses. *IEEE Transactions on Engineering Management, 70*(3), 950–962. https://doi.org/10.1109/TEM.2022.3167282

Gevorkyan, A. V. (2021, June 24). *Can diaspora bonds supercharge development investment?* Migration Information Source. Migration Policy Institute. https://www.migrationpolicy.org/article/diaspora-bonds-supercharge-development-investment

Gillespie, K., Riddle,L., Sayre, E., & Sturges, D. (1999). Diaspora homeland investment interest. *Journal of International Business Studies 30*(3), 623–634.

Giuliano, P., & Ruiz-Arranz, M. (2009). Remittances, financial development, and growth. *Journal of Development Economics, 90*(1), 144–152. https://doi.org/10.1016/j.jdeveco.2008.10.005

Kakhkharov, J. (2019). Migrant remittances as a source of financing for entrepreneurship. *International Migration, 57*(5), 37–55. https://doi.org/10.1111/imig.12531

Luqman, R., Kehinde Issa, A.-J., Owolabi, A. B., Yakub, A. O., Same, N. N., Yasin, N., Kavgic, M., Suh, D., & Huh, J.-S. (2023). Assessing the viability of a grid-connected PV power plant in Mubi, Adamawa State, Nigeria. *Frontiers in Energy Research, 11*. https://doi.org/10.3389/fenrg.2023.1205646

Nanziri, L. E., Zimuto, W., & Adjei-Mensah, G. (2025). Diaspora bonds and infrastructure finance. In G. Kararach, E. P. Moreira, & V. Murinde (Eds.), *The Palgrave handbook of development finance* (pp. 389–411). Palgrave Macmillan. https://doi.org/10.1007/978-3-031-77422-5_20

Owusu-Mante, S., Chi, K. H.-K., & Gopalakrishnan, T. (2025). *Sovereign green bonds in practice: Effectiveness as a climate finance instrument in emerging economies*. Climate Policy. Advance online publication. https://doi.org/10.1080/14693062.2025.2586572

Park, S., & Tuxhorn, K.-L. (2025). Investment across borders: How diaspora firms weigh financial returns and emotional-social drivers. *Asian and Pacific Migration Journal, 34*(4), 653–675. https://doi.org/10.1177/01171968251393548

Ratha, D., Plaza, S., & Kim, E. J. (2024, December 18). *In 2024, remittance flows to low- and middle-income countries are expected to reach $685 billion, larger than FDI and ODA combined*. People Move. World Bank Blogs. https://blogs.worldbank.org/en/peoplemove/in-2024--remittance-flows-to-low--and-middle-income-countries-ar

Rogge, E. (2025). Blue bonds: Sustainable financing for the Blue Economy around the Indian Ocean. *Jindal Global Law Review, 16*, 155–177. https://doi.org/10.1007/s41020-025-00263-5

Romagnoli, S., & Santini, A. (2025). *Climate risk and sovereign debt: Country-level exposures and scarcity effects in green bonds*. Decisions in Economics and Finance. Advance online publication. https://doi.org/10.1007/s10203-025-00554-5

Schneidman, W., Tadesse, A., & Lissanu, A. (2022, May 27). *Diaspora bonds: An innovative source of financing?* Brookings. https://www.brookings.edu/articles/diaspora-bonds-an-innovative-source-of-financing/

Sobiech, I. (2019). Remittances, finance and growth: Does financial development foster the impact of remittances on economic growth? *World Development, 113*, 44–59. https://doi.org/10.1016/j.worlddev.2018.08.016

Ul-Durar, S., De Sisto, M., Arshed, N., Yasin, N., & Reynolds, K. (2025). Natural capital productivity as a decoupler of energy and emissions in Sub-Saharan Africa. *Energy Economics, 145*, Article 108484. https://doi.org/10.1016/j.eneco.2025.108484

Vaaler, P. M. (2013). Diaspora concentration and the venture investment impact of remittances. *Journal of International Management, 19*(1), 26–46. https://doi.org/10.1016/j.intman.2012.11.004

Viglialoro, D., Botelho, T., Ughetto, E., Laspia, A., & Landoni, P. (2025). Social impact business angels as new impact investors. *British Journal of Management, 36*(2), 707–725. https://doi.org/10.1111/1467-8551.12864

Yasin, N. (2022). Cold Grass or Hot Sands: A Comparative Study of Immigrant Punjabi-Pakistani Entrepreneurs in London and Dubai. *Strategic Change: Briefings in Entrepreneurial Finance, 31*(4), 1–10.

Yasin, N., & Gilani, S. A. M. (2022). Assessing the current state of university-based business incubators in Canada. *Industry and Higher Education.* https://doi.org/10.1177/09504222221124749

Yasin, N., Gilani, S. A. M., Nair, G., Abaido, G. M., & Askri, S. (2023). Establishing a nexus for effective university-industry collaborations in the MENA region: A multi-country comparative study. *Industry and Higher Education.* https://doi.org/10.1177/09504222231175862

Yasin, N., Hafeez, K., Haq, M., Haq, F., Zahoor, N., & Noaman, S. (2026a). Take a break: A typology of immigrant enterprise growth strategies in non-traditional entrepreneurship settings. *Journal of Entrepreneurship in Emerging Economies.* https://doi.org/10.1108/JEEE-09-2025-0568

Yasin, N., Haq, M., Dana, L. P., & Salamzadeh, A. (2025a). "Try to keep them dumb and under the thumb": Exploring the "darker side" of psychological contracts in "overly embedded" immigrant enterprises. *Employee Relations, 47*(3/4), 537–556. https://doi.org/10.1108/ER-04-2024-0235

Yasin, N., Haq, M., Hafeez, K., & Zahoor, N. (2025b). Are some immigrant entrepreneurs more privileged than others? A cross-national comparison of financial capital among start-ups in the UK and UAE. *The Journal of Race, Ethnicity, and Politics*, 1–24. https://doi.org/10.1017/rep.2025.10031

Yasin, N., & Khansari, Z. (2021). Evaluating the impact of social enterprise education on students' enterprising characteristics in the United Arab Emirates. *Education + Training, 63*(6), 827–905.

Yasin, N., & Khansari, Z. (2022). Exploring the enterprise landscape for business incubators in the UAE. In D. Hyams-Ssekasi & F. Agboma (Eds.), *Entrepreneurship and Change.* Palgrave Macmillan. https://doi.org/10.1007/978-3-031-07139-3_8

Yasin, N., & Nabi, G. (2026). Entrepreneurship education in the United Arab Emirates: An extended resource-based view of institutional resources and contextual challenges in higher education. *International Journal of Entrepreneurial Behaviour and Research.* https://doi.org/10.1108/IJEBR-02-2025-0161

Yasin, N., Margaça, C., Haq, M., Poulin, M., & Salamzadeh, A. (2026b). The multi-capital playbook: Explaining immigrant entrepreneurship through the forms of capital. In C. Salloum, L.-P. Dana, A. Hasnaoui & M. Rossi (Eds.), *The immigrant entrepreneur's capital playbook: Green money, global talent, and the path to prosperity.* Springer Nature, Chapter 1.

Yasin, N., & Poulin, M. (2025). Developing a nation of entrepreneurs: The integral role of immigrant entrepreneurship for the United Arab Emirates Vision 2030. In C. Margaça, A. Walmsley, & H. Knörr (Eds.), *Immigrant entrepreneurship, religion, and ethnicity: Cases from Europe, Africa, and Asia* (pp. 187–204). Routledge. https://doi.org/10.4324/9781003489214-12

Zahoor, N., Usman, M., Khalid, A., Aboelmaged, M. G., & Yasin, N. (2025). *Green strategic intent, artificial intelligence capability, and behavioural dynamics for achieving circular economy goals in the public sector.* Technological Forecasting and Social Change.

ESG & Impact Measurement for Angel Portfolios

Roy Matta, Marion Polge, and Ruba Younes

Abstract The rapid mainstreaming of Environmental, Social, and Governance (ESG) considerations has transformed the investment landscape, yet their application to angel investing remains underexplored. This chapter addresses this gap by proposing a structured and evidence-based approach to integrating ESG criteria and impact measurement into early-stage investment portfolios. It contributes by bridging impact investing theory with the practical realities of angel portfolio management, offering a framework that supports both financial performance and measurable societal outcomes. The chapter first situates ESG and impact investing within the evolving angel investment ecosystem, highlighting key drivers such as regulatory developments, shifting investor expectations, and the rise of purpose-driven entrepreneurship. It then clarifies core ESG dimensions and demonstrates how their integration can enhance risk management, strategic positioning, and long-term value creation. Building on this foundation, the chapter examines how ESG factors can be embedded throughout the investment process, from screening and due diligence to portfolio construction and post-investment engagement. Practical tools and approaches are presented to help investors assess governance structures, environmental exposure, and social impact in early-stage ventures, while managing inherent trade-offs between financial returns and impact objectives. A central focus is placed on impact measurement, a critical yet complex component of responsible investing. The chapter reviews both qualitative and quantitative methodologies, including standardized frameworks such as IRIS + and the Sustainable Development Goals (SDGs), as well as customized indicators adapted to early-stage contexts. Key challenges such as data limitations, lack of standardization, and greenwashing risks are critically discussed, alongside pragmatic solutions. Finally, the chapter introduces a portfolio-level perspective on ESG and impact evaluation, emphasizing monitoring, reporting, and strategic optimization. By framing ESG integration as a dynamic and learning-oriented process, the chapter highlights its potential to strengthen portfolio resilience, attract aligned stakeholders, and foster sustainable innovation. This chapter positions ESG and impact measurement not as constraints but as strategic

R. Matta (✉) · M. Polge · R. Younes
USJ Business School, Saint Joseph University of Beirut, Beirut, Lebanon
e-mail: roy.matta@usj.edu.lb

H. Jarrar et al. (eds.), *Diaspora Angel Investing*, Ethnic and Indigenous Business Studies, https://doi.org/10.1007/978-3-032-33088-8_7

levers for value creation in angel investing, contributing to a new paradigm where financial performance and societal impact are jointly pursued.

1 Introduction

Angel investing has traditionally been synonymous with identifying the next high-growth venture. However, the landscape is evolving, as investors now face increasing pressure to consider how their capital aligns with broader societal goals such as environmental protection, social inclusion, and sound governance. This shift reflects a broader trend in which Environmental, Social, and Governance (ESG) and impact investing have evolved from niche practices into mainstream expectations, permeating public markets and institutional portfolios. These practices are now extending into early-stage finance, including business angel networks, where investors are being urged by regulators, limited partners, and entrepreneurs to integrate sustainability considerations into their decision-making processes and value creation models (Siefkes & Lahr, 2026). Against this backdrop, angel investors are emerging as key players in advancing sustainable innovation. Their unique position; working closely with founders and having the opportunity to influence business models; allows them to become important catalysts for sustainability at a stage where ESG considerations can be locked in. This growing influence of angel investors in the sustainable space is supported by recent research on green business angels, which shows how certain investors not only provide capital but also offer invaluable sustainability-specific expertise, networks, and legitimacy. These elements are crucial for helping startups navigate the complexities of accessing markets and securing follow-on financing. Additionally, the rise of social impact business angels underscores the transformation of angel investing from a purely financial pursuit to one that blends financial returns with a focus on social and environmental impact. This shift is challenging the traditional high-risk, high-return logic of early-stage investing and introducing new governance practices (Roor & Maas, 2024). Nevertheless, despite the rapid adoption of ESG language in the angel investing domain, critical questions persist regarding the true meaning of impact at the portfolio level. In particular, the challenge of defining, measuring, and evaluating impact in small, young ventures remains a pressing concern. Furthermore, investors face difficult decisions regarding the trade-offs between short-term financial returns and long-term societal outcomes. Evidence from emerging markets illustrates how impact investing is gaining traction but continues to grapple with fragmented metrics, limited data, and relatively small investment sizes. These challenges make it more difficult to robustly evaluate portfolios, especially when compared to the more established structures of private equity or public markets. This book chapter seeks to address these tensions by exploring how ESG and impact considerations can be systematically integrated into angel investing portfolios. It aims to guide investors through the processes of screening, due diligence, impact measurement, monitoring, and strategic portfolio optimization, eventually offering practical insights on how to reconcile financial and social objectives in early-stage investments (Olugbenga et al., 2025).

2 The Foundations of ESG and Impact Investing in Angel Portfolios

2.1 Defining ESG Criteria and Impact Metrics

Environmental, social, and governance (ESG) investing and impact investing emerged from older traditions of ethical and socially responsible investment, but they now form a distinct and rapidly professionalizing field. Early work on impact investing stresses intentionality; a deliberate commitment to generate measurable social and environmental outcomes alongside financial return; and highlights how the term crystallized in the late 2000s around the Global Impact Investing Network (GIIN) and related field-building efforts (Agrawal & Jespersen, 2024). In parallel, ESG investing evolved as mainstream capital markets started to integrate non-financial information on how firms manage environmental risks, labor and community relations, and governance structures. ESG analysis focuses on the how of corporate behavior; policies, processes, and risk management; whereas impact investing adds a why by tying capital deployment to precise impact objectives and theories of change (Bissoondoyal-Bheenick et al., 2024). ESG criteria are commonly organized into three pillars: environmental (such as carbon footprint, resource efficiency, pollution), social (such as employee welfare, diversity, community impact), and governance (such as board independence, shareholder rights, transparency). At a portfolio level, these criteria are used to screen, score, and sometimes engage with investee companies, with empirical work showing that firms with strong ESG profiles often display more stable earnings and risk profiles than peers. Impact investing adds a second layer by requiring that investors articulate ex ante impact intentions, track progress using clear metrics, and use that information in decision-making. The GIIN codifies this through four core elements known as intentionality, return expectations, a spectrum of financial performance, and impact measurement and management (IMM), which together differentiate impact investing from broader ESG or exclusionary screening (Abouarab et al., 2025). Over the past decade, a wide range of tools and standards have been developed to support IMM. Metric sets such as IRIS and ratings systems such as GIIRS, alongside frameworks like Social Return on Investment (SROI) and theory-of-change approaches, aim to make impact more comparable and auditable across funds and asset classes. These infrastructures matter for angel portfolios because they offer ready-made taxonomies and indicators that can be adapted to very early-stage ventures rather than starting from scratch. Yet measurement is far from straightforward. Reviews of impact investing and social impact investing emphasize persistent tensions between the desire for standardized, investor-friendly metrics and the contextual, qualitative nature of many social and environmental outcomes. Scholars also point to aggregate confusion in ESG ratings and the risk that over-reliance on external scores obscures the specific value-creation logics of individual ventures, especially at early stages (Andonov et al., 2025).

2.2 Why ESG and Impact Matter for Angel Investors

Angel investors sit at the earliest and riskiest end of the equity spectrum, where information is scarce and business models are still fluid, yet they increasingly operate in an environment where ESG and impact language shapes entrepreneurs' narratives, co-investors' expectations, and public policy priorities. Evidence on green business angels shows that a growing subset of angels clearly targets sustainability-oriented ventures and see themselves as allies of the ecological transition rather than purely financial arbitrageurs (Kathan et al., 2025). For these investors, ESG and impact considerations are not just a reputational add-on; they influence sourcing, screening, and post-investment engagement. Studies of impact investing decision processes highlight that investors look simultaneously at standard venture criteria; such as team quality, innovation, and market potential; and at the venture's mission, beneficiary focus, and capacity to deliver verifiable outcomes. Similar patterns appear in recent work on social impact business angels, who adopt clear impact theses, use tailored assessment grids, and often accept more patient capital structures in exchange for deeper societal results (Pimenta et al., 2024). There is also emerging evidence that ventures which credibly signal sustainability and social responsibility attract more attention from angels and improve their access to follow-on capital. A recent review of business angel research finds that signaling sustainability can increase the likelihood and scale of angel commitments, especially where angels perceive impact as synergistic with long-term financial performance. This creates tangible incentives for entrepreneurs to embed ESG practices early and to develop coherent impact narratives that resonate with potential backers (Iurkov et al., 2024). At a portfolio level, incorporating ESG and impact considerations can help angels manage risk and build resilience. Studies of ESG and impact funds show that high-ESG performers often exhibit lower earnings volatility and can contribute to more stable, diversified portfolios, even if headline returns sometimes differ from conventional benchmarks. For angels who typically hold highly concentrated, illiquid portfolios, using ESG and impact lenses to identify ventures with strong stakeholder relationships, regulatory preparedness, and long-term licence to operate can serve as an additional risk-mitigation layer (Fernandes Da Silva Ranchordas & Meoli, 2024). Finally, ESG and impact integration increasingly shapes the wider financing ecosystem that surrounds angel investors. Development finance institutions and public investors, for example, now routinely embed ESG requirements into their venture capital programs and work with fund managers to design ESG management systems, board practices, and reporting processes that cascade down to portfolio companies. Angels who align with these expectations are better positioned to syndicate with institutional co-investors, access blended-finance structures, and support their ventures through later funding rounds where ESG and impact disclosures become more formalized (Eckerle& Terzidis, 2025).

3 Integrating ESG Factors into Angel Investment Decision-Making

3.1 ESG as a Core Investment Filter and Screening Mechanism

ESG considerations have progressively shifted from being a peripheral concern to a central component of investment decision-making. Rather than functioning as a reputational or ethical add-on, ESG is increasingly integrated into risk-return analysis, with investors using non-financial information to enhance long-term performance and reduce exposure to regulatory, operational, and reputational risks. This evolution reflects a broader structural shift in capital allocation, where ESG-aligned strategies attract significant financial flows, influencing how early-stage investors, including angels, assess opportunities. In practice, this shift translates into earlier and more systematic engagement with ESG-related issues during the investment process (Heinz & Velamuri, 2024). Even in the absence of formal ESG scoring systems at the seed stage, angel investors implicitly evaluate governance quality, founder integrity, environmental exposure, and social impact when assessing business models and leadership teams. Weak governance structures or unsustainable practices are increasingly viewed as potential barriers to scaling, follow-on funding, and exit opportunities. Screening represents the first point of ESG integration. Angel investors increasingly apply both negative and positive screening criteria to shape deal flow. Negative screening excludes ventures operating in sectors such as fossil fuels, arms, or exploitative financial services; while positive screening prioritizes ventures addressing environmental sustainability, resource efficiency, or social inclusion challenges (Paques, 2024). This approach is particularly evident among green business angels, who seek measurable environmental or social outcomes alongside financial returns. Regulatory developments further reinforce ESG-oriented screening practices. Exposure to frameworks such as the Sustainable Finance Disclosure Regulation (SFDR) encourages investors to avoid business models that may later be classified as non-aligned, as this can affect portfolio liquidity and future exit opportunities (Nsama, 2025). As a result, ESG considerations are increasingly embedded not only in individual investment decisions but also in broader portfolio positioning strategies. Following initial screening, ESG due diligence deepens the analysis by examining how ventures manage environmental, social, and governance risks in practice. Early-stage adaptations of established frameworks, such as TCFD and SASB, guide assessments of legal compliance, environmental practices, labor conditions, data privacy, and diversity. Although formal site visits may be limited, structured interviews with founders and employees provide insights into resource use, supply chain risks, and regulatory exposure (Oliveira et al., 2025). Tools such as comprehensive ESG questionnaires demonstrate that even early-stage firms can be evaluated against standardized criteria, allowing benchmarking across key dimensions such as environmental policies, health and safety, and inclusion practices. A critical aspect of this process is distinguishing between symbolic ESG narratives and materially relevant factors that affect financial performance. Evidence shows that many startups possess fragmented ESG practices and limited measurement systems, even when they claim environmental or social impact. Investors must therefore assess the materiality of ESG issues in relation to specific business models (Rizzitello et al., 2025). For example, data-driven firms may face higher risks related to privacy and algorithmic bias, whereas industrial or hardware ventures are more exposed to environmental and supply chain risks. The relational nature of angel investing further shapes ESG integration. Investment decisions often depend on alignment between investors and founders regarding values, mission, and long-term vision. While investors hold initial decision power, they rely on founders' ongoing commitment to ESG principles after investment. Assessing intrinsic motivation, governance practices, and stakeholder engagement helps differentiate genuinely mission-driven ventures from those engaging in superficial impact washing (Chan, 2026). However, ESG integration at this stage is constrained by significant information gaps. Early-stage ventures typically lack standardized ESG data, and existing rating systems vary widely in methodology, creating inconsistencies and uncertainty. This lack of reliable data increases the risk of greenwashing and limits the effectiveness of purely quantitative approaches. As a result, angel investors often combine qualitative judgment with simple, transparent indicators rather than relying on complex scoring models designed for mature firms (Ruggeri et al., 2025).

3.2 ESG Integration at Portfolio and Post-Investment Levels

Beyond individual investment decisions, ESG integration shapes portfolio construction, performance expectations, and post-investment engagement. Angel investors exhibit diverse approaches to balancing financial returns and impact objectives, ranging from return-focused strategies that treat ESG primarily as a risk management tool to impact-driven approaches that prioritize social or environmental outcomes, even at the expense of financial returns. Many adopt a portfolio-level perspective, combining investments optimized for financial performance with others aligned with specific sustainability themes, thereby constructing a personalized impact-return balance (Huy & Dinh, 2025). At the portfolio level, ESG integration influences diversification strategies, sector focus, and risk management. Evidence from broader asset management contexts suggests that ESG-oriented portfolios may offer greater resilience and downside protection, although long-term performance effects remain debated. In early-stage investing, emerging research indicates that portfolios focused on sustainability and innovation can achieve competitive outcomes, provided that investors actively manage technological, regulatory, and market risks (Nayeem, 2026). Structured ESG evaluation tools and benchmarking practices further support portfolio-level decision-making by informing follow-on investments and engagement priorities. Regulatory considerations also extend to portfolio construction. For investors operating within frameworks such as SFDR, the classification of portfolio companies becomes critical, as a high proportion of non-aligned investments can reduce the attractiveness of the overall portfolio to institutional investors and limit access to future capital (Gupta et al., 2026). Consequently, ESG integration increasingly requires forward-looking portfolio design that anticipates both regulatory constraints and market expectations. ESG considerations also play a central role in post-investment stewardship. Angel investors often contribute beyond capital by providing mentorship, governance support, and access to networks. These value-adding activities are increasingly aligned with ESG objectives, as investors seek to influence the development of sustainable practices within portfolio companies. Effective stewardship involves setting clear ESG expectations at the investment stage, defining measurable objectives, and providing practical support through tools, training, and expert connections (Jin et al., 2026). Rather than imposing complex reporting requirements, successful approaches focus on building capabilities within early-stage firms, enabling them to integrate ESG considerations progressively as they scale. This includes developing governance structures, improving transparency, and embedding sustainability into business models. Investors who adopt this approach are more likely to select ventures where they can meaningfully influence outcomes, reinforcing the idea that ESG integration is not limited to screening out undesirable investments but extends to actively shaping the trajectory of portfolio companies. In general, ESG integration in angel investing represents a shift from isolated decision-making toward a holistic approach encompassing screening, due diligence, portfolio construction, and active stewardship. While challenges related to data availability, standardization, and measurement persist, the growing emphasis on ESG reflects a broader transformation in investment practices, where financial performance, risk management, and societal impact are increasingly interconnected (Fabozzi & Focardi, 2025).

4 Measuring Impact: Tools, Metrics, and Challenges

4.1 Quantitative and Qualitative Impact Assessment Methods

For angel investors, impact measurement is essential in connecting intentionality, capital allocation, and post-investment support to concrete evidence of change. Impact measurement and management (IMM) have become a key approach in impact investing, where investors define impact objectives, select indicators, track performance, and refine strategies. IMM anchors the four core pillars of impact investing known as intentionality, return expectations, asset class breadth, and measurement commitment. Frameworks like IRIS and global reporting standards offer a shared language for social and environmental performance, adaptable even to small, illiquid angel portfolios (Khuntia, 2025). From an angel's perspective, qualitative, process-based approaches are often the most useful. Tools like theory-of-change diagrams, impact logic models, and narrative outcome maps help founders and investors clarify how a venture expects to create change, mapping the causal chain from activities to outputs, outcomes, and long-term impact. These methods are particularly relevant at the pre-seed and seed stages, where robust data may be scarce but the logic and assumptions behind a business model can still be tested. Recent studies show that qualitative methods are effective in structuring impact due diligence and engaging founders in discussions about risks, externalities, and unintended consequences, even when metrics are approximate (Dyer et al., 2025). To add a quantitative layer, scorecard-based tools rate ventures across dimensions like environmental footprint, beneficiary reach, governance quality, and scalability, using simple scales that can be aggregated into an overall score. These tools, such as impact scorecards and multi-criteria impact compasses, help angel syndicates compare deals, prioritize their pipeline, and track progress over time. However, research warns that off-the-shelf scorecards often assume data availability that many startups lack, meaning angels need to customize templates and embrace subjectivity (Owan et al., 2024). A third approach involves synthetic indicators, which compress multiple impact dimensions into one or a few composite indices, inspired by ESG scoring in public markets. These indices provide a snapshot of a portfolio's impact profile, allowing investors to track changes and simulate the impact of new deals. However, creating composite indicators can oversimplify complex issues, potentially overlooking qualitative differences between ventures. Research emphasizes the need for careful design of these indices in angel settings, ensuring they do not mask important nuances (Ramamoorthy, 2025). Mainstream tools were initially developed for larger organizations, prompting research to develop practical instruments for early-stage ventures. Design-oriented studies propose lightweight tools that combine quantitative indicators with qualitative prompts, co-created with both founders and investors to minimize reporting burdens while providing decision-useful data (Novita & Edriani, 2024). Impact measurement must be integrated into broader performance-management systems. Drawing from management control theory, recent studies link impact tools to specific roles within an investor's control system. For example, IRIS-style indicators act as diagnostic controls to track progress, while sustainability reporting standards like GRI serve as boundary systems to set minimum acceptable practices. Regular strategy dialogues or board-level interactions function as interactive controls, helping investors and entrepreneurs adapt strategies in response to new information. This perspective sees impact metrics not as a static checklist but as part of an ongoing conversation about goals, risk appetite, and portfolio adjustments (Wathore, 2026). A final practical layer involves key performance indicators (KPIs) that integrate financial and impact considerations. In impact-focused portfolios, KPIs are used to select ventures, monitor progress, and decide on follow-on investments or exits. Evidence from impact-investing practice shows that well-designed KPIs help translate broad social and environmental objectives into measurable targets; such as the number of low-income customers served, CO_2 avoided, or jobs created in underserved regions; that can be tracked alongside financial metrics like revenue and cash flow. Studies show that the most effective KPI systems are those co-designed by investors and entrepreneurs, remaining flexible enough to evolve with the business model (Alifwansyah et al., 2025).

4.2 Overcoming Data and Standardization Challenges

Even when angel investors agree on what to measure, navigating a fragmented data landscape presents challenges. Research on ESG ratings in public markets reveals discrepancies between major rating agencies, influenced by differences in scope, measurement choices, and weighting schemes. These discrepancies lead to varying ESG scores for the same company, showing that ESG ratings are subjective and shaped by specific methodological decisions. For angel investors, who may rely on third-party ESG data for co-investments or sector benchmarks, this highlights the importance of understanding how these scores are constructed to avoid distorting portfolio-level impact assessments (Gudmundsdottir & Sigurjonsson, 2024). Attempts to standardize ESG assessments through aggregation have shown both potential and limitations. Studies comparing aggregation methods like simple averages or voting systems reveal that aggregated scores can reduce noise and identify broad patterns. However, they also show that methodological differences remain significant, especially in less regulated markets. For angels, who often lack access to multiple data providers for a single startup, this underscores the need for transparency in constructing internal impact scores and testing results against alternative assumptions (Fagbemi et al., 2025). Data challenges are particularly acute at the startup level. Early-stage ventures often operate with limited data, rely on proxies for outcome measures, and face volatility that complicates year-on-year comparisons. Complex tools and demanding reporting templates can become barriers to measurement, especially for small teams juggling product development, fundraising, and operations. This paradox means that ventures needing impact-oriented capital often struggle to meet sophisticated reporting requirements unless investors adapt tools and timelines to their specific context (Khalil et al., 2026). Design-science research on impact tools for startups suggests strategies to mitigate these barriers while improving data quality. One approach is to build modular tools with a core set of simple, relevant metrics, gradually adding complexity as the venture matures. Another strategy aligns impact indicators with data founders already track for operational reasons, such as user registration, energy consumption, or churn rates, avoiding the need for entirely new data systems. Pilot studies show that these approaches significantly increase the founders' willingness to engage with impact reporting, leading to more reliable data for investment decision-making (Gharpure, 2025). Qualitative research into impact investors' selection processes reveals that evaluation does not rely solely on metrics. Investors combine structured checklists with in-depth discussions about the entrepreneur's mission, governance, and stakeholder engagement.

For angel investors, whose relationships with founders are typically close and long-term, measurement serves as a tool to surface questions about who benefits, where risks lie, and how impact can scale, rather than as a mechanical decision-making rule. Insights from institutional investors, such as development finance institutions (DFIs), offer useful lessons for angel investors. DFIs frequently combine portfolio-wide indicators with deal-specific metrics, tailoring impact measurement to each project's unique context. This hybrid approach provides comparability across deals while allowing flexibility for bespoke indicators that reflect each investee's theory of change (Yunus & Nanda, 2024). At the micro-level, research on green angels highlights how data challenges are intertwined with capacity-building. Business angels specializing in environmental ventures help founders interpret indicators, refine what to measure, and connect measurement to strategic decisions such as market selection or technology pathways. These angels supply capital while co-creating the impact measurement infrastructure that makes ESG and impact measurement meaningful. Regulatory developments further complicate data and standardization challenges. Analyses of the European Union's sustainable-finance framework show that while disclosure rules and sustainability labels channel funds toward ESG-branded investments, they risk creating new forms of greenwashing if applied without nuance (Ben Mahjoub, 2025). For smaller investors like angel networks, the challenge is to align with emerging taxonomies and disclosure standards without replicating frameworks designed for large companies. Scholars argue that selective adoption of relevant regulatory elements, coupled with ongoing dialogue, is crucial for ensuring compliance efforts strengthen real impact creation. Across these different strands of research, key design principles for angels seeking to measure ESG and impact credibly emerge. Metrics should be grounded in a clear causal story about how the investee creates change. Indicator sets should balance simplicity and coverage, measurement systems must be transparent and flexible, and investors should treat measurement as a shared responsibility, co-invested in alongside their portfolio companies (Bezerra et al., 2024).

5 Portfolio Evaluation and Optimization

5.1 Monitoring and Reporting ESG and Impact Performance

Angel investors who integrate ESG and impact considerations increasingly treat portfolio evaluation as a continuous management process rather than a box-ticking exercise at entry. For early-stage deals, the absence of long financial histories makes non-financial indicators even more central, which pushes angels to define a small set of core ESG and impact metrics that can be tracked consistently over time at company and portfolio levels. These metrics typically combine outcomes or output-based indicators (such as tons of CO_2 avoided, underserved customers reached, or percentage of women in leadership) with governance and process indicators that capture how seriously founders embed ESG in daily decision-making (Xidonas & Essner, 2024). In practice, many angels start with whatever impact narratives founders present, then gradually formalize reporting into structured templates and dashboards. Design-oriented work on impact assessment for entrepreneurship support organizations, shows how co-creation with founders can translate vague intentions into clear impact logics, indicators, data sources, and reporting routines that remain manageable for small teams. Such tools emphasize proportionality, asking early-stage ventures to focus on a handful of material indicators linked to their theory of change rather than broad ESG checklists designed for listed firms. For portfolios with multiple ventures and sectors, standardized taxonomies such as IRIS + or SDG mappings help angels aggregate impact information and identify where their capital is really flowing, but they rarely work off the shelf in pre-revenue contexts (Alabi, 2024). Evidence from impact investing funds shows that performance management systems work best when they combine top-down reference frameworks with bottom-up tailoring, so that each venture reports on indicators that are both comparable across the portfolio and meaningful for its specific business model. Green business angels highlight an additional monitoring dimension, the need to follow not only what ventures deliver but how they deliver it. Their sustainability value-adding activities often include challenging founders on the credibility of impact claims, negotiating concrete milestones for environmental and social performance, and requesting regular non-financial reports that are sufficiently granular to detect mission drift or greenwashing. This kind of engaged monitoring turns ESG from a static rating into an ongoing dialogue centered on learning and accountability between investor and founder (Taheripour et al., 2025). Systematic monitoring depends on robust underlying data, yet ESG measurement at venture level remains noisy and incomplete. Work on aggregating ESG ratings at the listed-firm level shows that different providers can disagree substantially on a company's ESG performance, and that portfolio outcomes are sensitive to how individual scores are combined into a single index. For angels who rely on external ESG signals; for example, when co-investing with funds or tracking later-stage performance; these findings underline the need to understand the construction of ESG scores and to avoid treating them as objective truth (Abate et al., 2024). As digital tools spread through the venture ecosystem, some investors experiment with integrating ESG and impact data directly into financial models, valuation spreadsheets, and CRM systems. Evidence from venture capital suggests that collecting ESG data from portfolio companies and feeding it into scenario analysis; such as adding ESG modifiers to revenue projections or adjusting discount rates for regulatory and reputational risk; can improve the realism of financial forecasts and strengthen conversations with later-stage investors about the link between ESG performance and exit potential (Gaurav et al., 2025).

5.2 Strategic Approaches for Portfolio Diversification and Growth

At a portfolio level, angels face a multi-dimensional optimization problem. They must balance risk, financial performance, and impact across a small number of highly uncertain bets. Studies of impact-oriented investment funds show that performance management tools can support this process by clarifying which impact themes, business models, or geographies generate both strong mission alignment and acceptable risk-return profiles, and by flagging concentrations that might threaten resilience. For individual angels, even simple dashboards that display exposure by impact theme, stage, or region can trigger strategic conversations about where to add or reduce positions (Vasuki et al., 2025). Research on green business angels and sustainable start-up finance suggests that many investors deliberately diversify across different environmental and social challenges (such as energy transition, circular economy, or social inclusion) rather than concentrating on a single niche. This diversification can reduce mission risk; if one policy domain stalls, other themes can still advance the investor's overarching purpose; while also creating opportunities for synergies and cross-pollination between ventures addressing adjacent parts of the same system (Ntare et al., 2025). Angel portfolios are typically small in absolute numbers, which makes each deal choice critical. Comparative work on business angels shows that investors who treat their portfolio as a learning laboratory; systematically reflecting on past exits and failures, adjusting their screening criteria, and refining the balance between sectors and stages over time; tend to converge toward more coherent strategies. In an ESG and impact context, this often means prioritizing ventures where investors can add non-financial value on ESG issues, rather than simply scattering capital across many impact labels without the capacity to support them (Purwanto et al., 2024). Another strategic dimension concerns syndication and collaboration with funds and other angels. Studies of green angel networks emphasize that co-investment structures can leverage specialized sustainability competences; such as technical expertise in renewable energy, regulatory know-how, or experience with impact measurement tools; that no single investor holds alone. When these networks share impact frameworks and reporting expectations, they create quasi-standards that reduce transaction costs for founders and enable more consistent portfolio-level analysis across co-investors (FROLOV et al., 2025). The quality of ESG and impact data has direct implications for portfolio optimization. Evidence from listed markets shows that aggregate ESG scores depend strongly on how disparate ratings are combined, and that disagreement across providers can materially affect the apparent performance of ESG-tilted portfolios. Angels attempting to compare or rebalance their holdings based on ESG profiles face similar challenges; if metrics are not constructed consistently, apparent leaders and laggards may simply reflect methodological noise rather than real differences in sustainability performance (Ahmar et al., 2025). In response, some venture and growth investors integrate ESG data collection into their value-creation plans, using ESG indicators not just for external reporting but as operational levers. A case material on ESG integration in start-up portfolios shows that investors can, for example, agree ESG roadmaps at investment, embed relevant KPIs in board reporting, and reassess valuations or follow-on decisions in light of ESG progress or backsliding. This approach turns portfolio optimization into a dynamic process that links capital allocation, founder support, and progressive tightening of sustainability expectations over the life of the investment. Finally, ESG and impact-oriented angels will judge portfolio success along at least three axes; preservation and growth of financial capital, achievement of measurable positive outcomes, and contribution to broader ecosystem change. Performance management frameworks developed for impact funds highlight that these axes need not be perfectly aligned at every deal, instead, investors can use a portfolio lens to combine higher-risk, high-impact experiments with more mature, financially robust ventures, and to accept different mixes of financial and impact performance across individual holdings as long as the overall portfolio remains coherent with its stated mandate (Moreira et al., 2026).

6 Conclusion

Angel investing is entering a new era where ignoring ESG (Environmental, Social, and Governance) and impact considerations is no longer a neutral option but a strategic disadvantage. As sustainable assets increasingly dominate global assets under management (AUM) and impact investing demonstrates the potential for achieving risk-adjusted returns alongside tangible real-world change, business angels face mounting pressure to clearly outline how their portfolios contribute to environmental resilience, social inclusion, and sound governance, rather than relying on informal judgments about responsible founders. This chapter has highlighted that angels occupy a unique position in the capital spectrum, often being the first institutionalized investors in a venture. They work closely with founders and influence strategy long before larger investors or regulators become involved, giving them significant leverage to embed ESG expectations into screening, term sheets, board conversations, and hands-on support for green and socially-oriented ventures (Santos et al., 2024). However, the realities of early-stage investing; thin data, evolving business models, and shifting materiality; mean that rigid, public-markets-style ESG checklists are often unsuitable. Effective angel investors strike a balance between structured due diligence and a contextual understanding of founder intent, stakeholder relationships, and the potential for professionalizing impact as the company grows. Looking forward, the frontier for ESG and impact in angel investing lies less in creating ever-more-complex labels and more in developing lean, learning-oriented measurement systems that are transparent about what can and cannot be quantified, connect impact metrics to investment decisions, and remain adaptable to the needs of pre-revenue startups (Espiga-Fernández et al., 2024). Emerging tools for startup impact assessment and performance management offer practical starting points, but persistent divergences in rating methodologies and standardization challenges indicate that achieving consistent, universal impact measures will remain a moving target for years to come. In this evolving landscape, angels who treat ESG and impact measurement as a disciplined, ongoing learning process; rather than a one-off compliance task; will be best positioned to attract aligned co-investors, navigate increasingly stringent regulations, and help build the next generation of ventures whose success will be defined not only by financial exits but by the lasting problems they solve (Wang et al., 2024).

References

Abate, G., Basile, I., & Ferrari, P. (2024). The integration of environmental, social and governance criteria in portfolio optimization: An empirical analysis. *Corporate Social Responsibility and Environmental Management, 31*(3), 2054–2065.

Abouarab, R., Mishra, T., & Wolfe, S. (2025). Does the EU sustainable finance disclosure regulation mitigate greenwashing? *The European Journal of Finance, 31*(8), 957–989.

Agrawal, A., & Jespersen, K. (2024). How do impact investors evaluate an investee social enterprise? A framework of impact investing process. *Journal of Entrepreneurship in Emerging Economies, 16*(4), 999–1022.

Ahmar, A. S., Wahyuni, W., Triutomo, A., Rahman, A., & Tabash, M. (2025). Cross-Sectoral portfolio optimization in emerging markets: Value at risk assessment of Indonesian consumer and financial stocks. *Quantitative Economics and Management Studies, 6*(1), 88–98.

Alabi, M. (2024). Social entrepreneurship: Balancing social impact and financial sustainability. *Journal of Social Entrepreneurship Research, 12*(3), 45–67.

Alifwansyah, A., Al Musadieq, M., Arifin, Z., & Worokinasih, S. (2025). A systematic review of firm sustainability metrics: Analytical approaches to performance and impact assessment. *KnE Social Sciences, 10*(13), 118–133.

Andonov, A., Li, A., & Smeets, P. (2025). Do development financial institutions create impact through venture capital investments? *Journal of International Development, 37*(2), 183–206.

Ben Mahjoub, L. (2025). Greenwashing practices and ESG reporting: An international review. *International Journal of Sociology and Social Policy, 45*(1–2), 173–188.

Bezerra, R. R. R., Martins, V. W. B., & Macedo, A. N. (2024). Validation of challenges for implementing ESG in the construction industry considering the context of an emerging economy country. *Applied Sciences, 14*(14), 6024.

Bissoondoyal-Bheenick, E., Bennett, S., Lehnherr, R., & Zhong, A. (2024). ESG rating disagreement: Implications and aggregation approaches. *International Review of Economics & Finance, 96*(1), Article 103532.

Chan, E. Y. (2026). Moral signaling in startups: How ESG claims shape stakeholder judgments and ethical legitimacy. *Journal of Business Ethics, 203*(2), 297–311.

Dyer, S., Hyder, C., & Kraemer, J. (2025). Challenges of key performance indicators and metrics for measuring medical science liaison performance: Insights from a global survey. *Pharmacy, 13*(2), 51.

Eckerle, C., & Terzidis, O. (2025). From ambition to evidence—A practical tool for startup impact assessment: C. Eckerle and O. Terzidis. *Small Business Economics, 18*(1), 1–20.

Espiga-Fernández, F., García-Sánchez, Á., & Ordieres-Meré, J. (2024). A systematic approach to portfolio optimization: A comparative study of reinforcement learning agents, market signals, and investment horizons. *Algorithms, 17*(12), 570.

Fabozzi, F. J., & Focardi, S. (2025). Integrating sustainability into asset management: Challenges and opportunities. *Journal of Portfolio Management, 51*(7), Article p95.

Fagbemi, B. T., Saah, B. P., Nduka, A. I., & Aloke, E. M. (2025). The evolution of ESG and sustainability reporting: A review of standards, challenges, and impacts on corporate transparency. *Journal of Economics, Business, and Commerce, 2*(2), 297–305.
Fernandes Da Silva Ranchordas, S. H., & Meoli, R. (2024). Regulatory sandboxes for sustainable finance. *Law and Economics Yearly Review, 13*(2), 243-280.
Frolov, A., Boiko, R., Rudevska, V., Butenko, D., & Moisiiakha, A. (2025). Evaluating modern quantitative methods for investment portfolio management under market uncertainty. *Journal of Applied Economic Sciences, 20*(3), 427–448.
Gaurav, A., Baishnab, K., & Singh, P. K. (2025). Intelligent ESG portfolio optimization: A multi-objective AI-driven framework for sustainable investments in the Indian stock market. *Sustainable Futures, 9*(1), Article 100832.
Gharpure, A. (2025). ESG reporting in enterprise financial systems: Challenges and innovations. *Journal of Computer Science and Technology Studies, 7*(3), 194–201.
Gudmundsdottir, S., & Sigurjonsson, T. O. (2024). A need for standardized approaches to manage sustainability strategically. *Sustainability, 16*(6), 2319.
Gupta, P., Jindal, A., Manjari, M., Gupta, R., Jain, A., Budhiraja, M., & Kumar, R. (2026). ESG (Environmental, Social, Governance) investment analytics for sustainable portfolio optimization. *Advances in Consumer Research, 3*(2), Article p433.
Heinz, D. C., & Velamuri, V. K. (2024). Intentionality and decision-making in impact investing; understanding investment motivation and selection criteria of impact investors. *Sustainability, 16*(11), 4497.
Huy, N. Q., & Dinh, L. Q. (2025). Balancing bank profits with sustainable development goals: Examining the pivotal role of financial stability. *Sustainable Development, 33*(1), 1182–1199.
Iurkov, V., Koval, M., Misra, S., Pedada, K., & Sinha, A. (2024). Impact of ESG distinctiveness in alliances on shareholder value. *Journal of Business Research, 171*(1), Article 114395.
Jin, L., Tsakalos, I., & Gkonis, V. (2026). ESG investing strategies: A bibliometric and systematic review. *Development and Sustainability in Economics and Finance, 9*(1), Article 100124.
Kathan, M. C., Utz, S., Dorfleitner, G., Eckberg, J., & Chmel, L. (2025). What you see is not what you get: ESG scores and greenwashing risk. *Finance Research Letters, 74*(1), Article 106710.
Khalil, M. K., Ali, M., & Ekşi, İ. H. (2026). Data analytics and ESG reporting: trends and challenges.
Khuntia, R. (2025). Measuring social impact: Metrics for evaluating social enterprises. *Global Dimensions of Multidisciplinary Research, 21*(1), 21–32.
Moreira, L., Santos, I. L. D., & Gonzalez, P. H. (2026). Portfolio optimization for pension purposes: literature review. *Journal of Economic Surveys, 40*(1), 45–72.
Nayeem, M. A. (2026). Environmental, Social, Governance (ESG) driven portfolio optimization integrating sustainability into investment decisions. *Advances in Consumer Research, 3*(1), Article p1358.
Novita, W., & Edriani, D. (2024). Measuring employee performance in the age of remote work: Key metrics and challenges. *Escalate: Economics and Business Journal, 2*(02), 54–65.
Nsama, F. (2025). Development of sustainable finance strategies for climate-resilient infrastructure investments across US States. *Communication in Physical Sciences, 12*(6), 1785–1813.
Ntare, H. B., Muteba Mwamba, J. W., & Adekambi, F. (2025). Dynamic portfolio optimization with diversification analysis and asset selection amidst high correlation using cryptocurrencies and bank equities. *Risks, 13*(6), 113.
Oliveira, A. Y., Mendes, J. A. J., Zanon, L. G., Gerolamo, M. C., & Zuin Zeidler, V. G. (2025). Sustainable Development: Prioritizing Attributes and Validating Factors for the Success of Green Startups in Brazilian and German Entrepreneurial Ecosystems. *Business Strategy & Development, 8*(1), e70083.
Olugbenga, A. F., Bali, O. J., Ofoama, C., Aluko, O. R., Aladesanmi, A., & Adeiza, L. A. (2025). The evolution of impact investing: Measuring social and financial returns across sectors. *Asian Business Research Journal, 10*(7), 76–91.

Owan, V. J., Agama, V. U., Odey, J. O., & Idika, D. O. (2024). Metrics in research impact assessment and grant funding: Insights from researchers in the" reviewer 2 must be stopped!" Facebook group. *Journal of Applied Learning & Teaching, 7*(1), 214–225.

Paques, A. (2024). Performance management tools in support of impact investing within investment funds. *Journal of Business Ethics, 189*(2), 451–471.

Pimenta, S., Duarte, A. P., & Simões, E. (2024). How socially responsible human resource management fosters work engagement: The role of perceived organizational support and affective organizational commitment. *Social Responsibility Journal, 20*(2), 326–343.

Purwanto, B., Respati, P., & Amanah, N. K. (2024). Optimal portfolio and the integrated strategy. *Management Analysis Journal, 13*(2), 130–139.

Ramamoorthy, L. (2025). Evaluating generative AI: Challenges, methods, and future directions. *International Journal of Future Multidisciplinary Research, 7*(1), 1–7.

Ruggeri, M., Vinci, G., Ruggieri, R., & Savastano, M. (2025). Facing the risk of greenwashing in the ESG report of global companies: The importance of life cycle thinking. *Corporate Social Responsibility and Environmental Management, 32*(3), 4216–4234.

Rizzitello, E., Piazza, M., & Perrone, G. (2025). Unlocking green startup investments: How environmental policy pressures drive venture capital funding decisions. *Technological Forecasting & Social Change, 217*(12415), 8.

Roor, A., & Maas, K. (2024). Do impact investors live up to their promise? A systematic literature review on (im) proving investments' impacts. *Business Strategy and the Environment, 33*(4), 3707–3732.

Santos, G. C., Barboza, F., Veiga, A. C. P., & de Souza, K. G. (2024). Portfolio optimization using artificial intelligence: A systematic literature review. *Exacta, 22*(3), 766–787.

Siefkes, M., & Lahr, K. (2026). Trust, gut feeling, and life cycle assessment: Angel approaches to sustainability impact assessments. *Venture Capital, 24*(1), 1–29.

Taheripour, E., Sadjadi, S. J., & Amiri, B. (2025). A multi-criteria approach to ESG-based portfolio optimization incorporating historical performance, forward-looking insights, and credibilistic CVaR: A case study on the DJIA. *Scientific Reports, 15*(1), 39088.

Vasuki, M., Celestin, M., Boakye, M. M., & Kumar, A. D. (2025). Evaluating the efficiency of portfolio diversification strategies using statistical correlation metrics. *Brainae Journal of Business, Sciences and Technology, 9*(2), 160–170.

Wang, A., Kresta, A., & Tichý, T. (2024). Evaluation of strategy portfolios: A. Wang et al. *Computational Management Science, 21*(1), 17.

Wathore, A. R. (2026). Research metrics and and academic evalution: Trends and challenges. *AIJMR-Advanced International Journal of Multidisciplinary Research, 4*(2), 1–5.

Xidonas, P., & Essner, E. (2024). On ESG portfolio construction: A multi-objective optimization approach. *Computational Economics, 63*(1), 21–45.

Yunus, Y. A., & Nanda, S. (2024). Exploring sustainable finance: A qualitative inquiry into responsible investment and ESG risk evaluation. *Golden Ratio of Finance Management, 4*(1), 01–13.

Country Dashboards for Diaspora Angel Investing: Comparing Corridors, Sectors, and Instrument Fit

L.' Hocine Houanti

Abstract This chapter develops an evidence-based way to compare diaspora investment corridors without reducing them to simplistic country rankings. Drawing research on diaspora investment, entrepreneurship, foreign direct investment, and cross-border angel finance, it argues that a useful dashboard must look at more than diaspora size or remittance volume. It must also consider institutional reliability, sector pipeline depth, exit options, and the fit between a corridor and the financing instrument being used. Using examples from India, Korea, South Africa–Europe, Cyprus–Israel, and the Balkan region, the chapter shows why the same pool of diaspora capital behaves differently across countries and sectors. The analysis then explains how investors and policymakers can use dashboard logic to choose between angel rounds, syndicates, SPVs, blended vehicles, and larger project finance tools. The result is a mature synthesis that turns comparative evidence into practical screening discipline.

1 Introduction

General discussions of diaspora investment often flatten geography. They speak as if diaspora capital were a single resource waiting to be mobilized once governments launch the right campaign. The evidence points in a different direction. Diaspora investors respond to corridor-specific combinations of familiarity, institutional reliability, sector opportunity, policy design, and expected returns. A country with a large diaspora may still be a poor fit for early-stage angel investing if exit options are weak or legal friction is high. Another country may attract less sentiment but deliver much better outcomes because the instrument, sector, and corridor are better aligned.

That distinction matters for this book project because investor-side playbooks are only useful when they travel across real contexts. The same diaspora capital might be well suited to seed-stage exportable software in one corridor, growth-stage healthcare in another, and climate-linked project vehicles in a third. It may also be

L. H. Houanti (✉)
EM Normandie Business School, Le Havre, France
e-mail: lhouanti@em-normandie.fr

H. Jarrar et al. (eds.), *Diaspora Angel Investing*, Ethnic and Indigenous Business Studies, https://doi.org/10.1007/978-3-032-33088-8_8

better deployed through FDI, an SPV, or a bond rather than through angel equity. The task, then, is not to produce a superficial ranking of countries. It is to build a dashboard that helps investors compare corridors in a disciplined way and match the right instrument to the right setting.

This chapter offers such a dashboard. It draws on the diaspora-investment literature, cross-border angel research, and selected country cases embedded in the uploaded source pack. The result is comparative and practical. It shows how a few evidence-based dimensions can materially improve pipeline screening and prevent the common error of treating diaspora identity as a stand-alone investment thesis.

The dashboard approach also answers a writing problem common in this field. Comparative work on diaspora capital can become either too anecdotal or too macro. It either tells memorable stories without giving investors a decision rule, or it presents large aggregates that say very little about how a real deal should be structured. A corridor dashboard sits between those extremes. It uses comparative evidence to sharpen investment judgment while preserving the contextual texture that diaspora finance always requires.

2 What a Useful Country Dashboard Should Measure

A useful dashboard begins by refusing the obvious but incomplete metrics. Diaspora size matters. Remittance volume matters. Neither is enough. Large diasporas can produce weak investment if trust in domestic institutions is low, if investable pipelines are shallow, or if the prevailing vehicle does not fit the country's corporate and regulatory realities. Park (2021) shows that diaspora engagement policies are not uniformly effective; their impact depends on the conditions under which they operate. Ragazzi (2014) reaches a similar conclusion from a policy-comparison angle, showing that diaspora strategies vary markedly in purpose, institutionalization, and reach.

For investors, five dimensions are especially useful. The first is familiarity: not simply emotional attachment, but the extent to which diaspora members can interpret local signals accurately. Leblang (2010) and Tong (2005) show that diaspora and ethnic networks can reduce information and transaction costs in cross-border investment. The second is institutional reliability: contract enforcement, bureaucratic predictability, foreign-exchange management, and the practical ease of operating a company. The third is sector depth: whether the country has enough genuine deal flow in the sectors diaspora investors are most likely to understand and support. The fourth is exit and follow-on capacity. The fifth is instrument fit: whether angel equity, an SPV, a blended vehicle, or larger-scale debt is the more natural tool for the corridor in question.

That framework matters because it forces investors to compare like with like. A country can be strong on familiarity and weak on exits. Another can have moderate familiarity but strong sector depth and cleaner legal infrastructure. A third can attract large remittances but be much better suited to project finance or growth capital than to early-stage angel rounds. Dizo-Conteh et al. (2025) and Riddle et al. (2010) both show that diaspora networks create value by bridging institutional divides. A good dashboard therefore asks not whether the diaspora is engaged, but what exactly the diaspora can bridge—and where the remaining gap is still too large.

What emerges is a more disciplined way of thinking about fit. Countries should not be ranked as universally good or bad for diaspora capital. They should be assessed relative to the form of capital under consideration.

A well-built dashboard should therefore combine public indicators with deal-level evidence. Macro data on remittances, migration stocks, and investment flows are useful starting points, but they need to be read alongside evidence on actual transaction frictions, sector performance, founder quality, and the local availability of follow-on capital. Otherwise, countries with impressive headline numbers may look artificially attractive, while smaller but better structured corridors are overlooked. The quality of the dashboard depends not on how many indicators it contains, but on whether those indicators help investors distinguish opportunity from sentiment.

Some investors prefer to turn dashboards into scores. That can be helpful as a first filter, but it should never replace narrative judgment. A corridor may score modestly on aggregate indicators yet still be highly attractive for one sector because diaspora investors have unusual commercial reach there. Another corridor may look strong on remittance data and policy symbolism but remain unsuitable for seed-stage equity because later capital is missing. Dashboards are strongest when they help investors ask sharper questions, not when they invite false precision.

Weighting those dimensions is itself a strategic choice. An investor focused on pre-seed software may prioritize sector depth and follow-on visibility over macro remittance size. An investor interested in project-linked climate vehicles may care more about policy credibility and institutional execution than about startup exits. The dashboard is useful precisely because it can be recalibrated around the capital form being considered. That flexibility is one of its advantages over one-size-fits-all national rankings.

3 Corridor Contrasts Across Regions

India offers one kind of corridor logic. It combines a very large diaspora-linked financial base with a more established entrepreneurial-finance ecosystem than many emerging markets. Ratha et al. (2024) estimate remittances to India at $129 billion in 2024, while historical work shows the long-standing developmental significance of diaspora-linked finance in the country (Ye, 2014). That does not make every Indian startup easy to price or fund. It does mean that diaspora capital can plug into a deeper set of local angels, accelerators, and later-stage investors than is available in many thinner markets. In such a corridor, angel syndicates and SPVs can be effective because they connect to a wider follow-on environment rather than operating in isolation (Mustafa, 2021).

Korea illustrates a different pattern. Park and Tuxhorn (2025) show that homeland-oriented diaspora firms do not abandon financial logic. Non-material motivations help when expected returns are broadly competitive, but they do not compensate for clearly inferior economics. That result is more useful than it first appears. It suggests that the Korean corridor may support diaspora-backed investment where strategic, technological, or commercial complementarities are already visible, yet it is unlikely to reward purely symbolic homeland appeals. The dashboard lesson is that some corridors are highly responsive to co-investment and strategic alignment, but not to patriotic discounting.

The South Africa–Europe corridor offers another contrast. Mestwerdt et al. (2025) show how severe contextual information asymmetries shape signaling between South African founders and European business angels. The opportunity is real, but so is the risk of misreading signals across institutional and cultural distance. In this kind of corridor, the dashboard should weight intermediaries, external validation, and syndication heavily. The issue is not a lack of opportunity. It is the cost of interpretation. Angel equity remains viable, but only when the bridge between local knowledge and foreign investor judgment is strong enough.

Cyprus, viewed through Israeli and Jewish diaspora investment, highlights yet another pattern. Kontakos and Stavrou (2025) report that Israeli FDI stock in Cyprus reached €920 million in 2021, nearly 54 percent above the previous year, while broader diaspora-linked investment also touched sectors such as real estate, financial services, hospitality, and technology. This is not primarily an early-stage angel story. It is a corridor where legal structure, tax treatment, gateway positioning, and sector-specific entry modes strongly influence outcomes. The dashboard implication is clear: some diaspora corridors look attractive on familiarity and business infrastructure, but their natural instrument may be FDI, holding-company structures, or project vehicles more often than classic seed rounds.

Balkan economies provide a final contrast. Schmutzler et al. (2021) show that diaspora actors can play a meaningful role in opportunity-driven entrepreneurial ecosystems, but the strength of the effect depends on the wider ecosystem's ability to absorb diaspora resources productively. Here, intermediary quality and local ecosystem depth matter at least as much as diaspora enthusiasm. The best opportunities may be export-oriented SMEs and service businesses that can use diaspora market access rather than purely domestic startups with weak scaling pathways. Once again, the corridor is investable—but only in a particular way.

African returnee and diaspora evidence adds a further reminder that the corridor itself can be more informative than the country label. Nyame-Asiamah et al. (2020) show that returnees investing in Africa respond to a mix of institutional push and pull factors rather than a simple homeland impulse. Ojo et al. (2013) similarly show that African diaspora entrepreneurs navigate entrepreneurial spaces across home and host countries at once. This means that dashboards should pay attention to the host-side capabilities of diaspora investors as well as the home-side characteristics of the target market. The bridge is made of both ends, not one.

Instrument choice can also differ sharply inside the same broad geographic region. A corridor with strong diaspora sentiment but weak startup exits may still be viable for project vehicles, diaspora notes, or structured FDI. By contrast, a corridor with less sentiment but deeper entrepreneurial finance may be superior for angel syndicates and SPVs. This is why comparing corridors only on identity or migration history misses the main investment point. The relevant comparison is between corridor conditions and financing tool, not between national stories alone.

The same logic helps explain why diaspora bonds, project vehicles, and angel equity should not be discussed as interchangeable across corridors. India's scale and financing depth make multiple forms viable. Korea's evidence points toward commercially disciplined diaspora participation rather than emotional overpricing. South Africa–Europe rewards structured signaling and syndication. Cyprus–Israel points toward gateway and FDI logic more than generic angelism. Balkan corridors may reward smaller, intermediary-supported plays. Once these differences are stated plainly, corridor choice becomes far more actionable. Table 1 compares selected diaspora investment corridors by fit, friction, and instrument choice.

4 Sector Fit Matters as Much as Country Fit

Country dashboards become much more useful when they are read through sectors rather than in the abstract. A country that is weak for local consumer apps may be strong for exportable healthcare services, logistics platforms, clean-tech distribution, or B2B software. Dizo-Conteh et al. (2025) and Yasin and Hafeez (2023) show that diaspora networks can be especially valuable when they help adapt products, open markets, and validate demand across borders. Those benefits are easier to realize in sectors where knowledge, trust, and market access travel. They are harder to realize where value depends mainly on a deep domestic consumer market or a dense local acquirer base that the country does not yet possess.

This is one reason why returnee and diaspora entrepreneurship in Africa often concentrates in sectors with clearer transnational linkages. Nyame-Asiamah et al. (2020) show that institutional push and pull factors shape diaspora entrepreneurs' investment decisions in Africa, while Ojo et al. (2013) document how African diaspora entrepreneurs navigate both home and host spaces rather than operating in one market alone. The practical reading is that sector selection and corridor selection should be made together. Investors should ask whether diaspora advantages are likely to show up in customer acquisition, talent access, supply-chain coordination, regulatory navigation, or export channels. If the answer is no, homeland familiarity may not materially improve the economics of the deal.

The climate and impact space adds another layer. Botelho et al. (2023) show that green angel investing is real but heterogeneous. Investors differ in how they balance economic, altruistic, and identity-based motives. This suggests that a country with a persuasive climate narrative is not automatically investable for green early-stage capital. It still needs a sector pipeline, credible policy support, and plausible follow-on finance. In some places climate opportunity will point toward project-linked vehicles

Table 1 Comparative dashboard for selected diaspora investment corridors

Corridor	Strongest near-term fit	Primary friction	Most suitable vehicle	Anchor evidence
India–global diaspora	Tech, digital services, health, climate-enabling ventures	Valuation stretch and selective follow-on capital	Angel syndicates, SPVs, co-investment funds	Large remittance base and deeper finance ecosystem
Korea–global diaspora	Strategic and technology-linked investments	Economic incentives must remain competitive	Co-investment and strategically aligned angel rounds	Non-material motives help only when returns are comparable
South Africa–Europe	Fintech, B2B, health, export-oriented ventures	Signal distortion and due-diligence cost	Lead-led syndicates with external validation	High cross-context information asymmetry
Cyprus–Israel/ Jewish diaspora	Gateway services, tech, hospitality, real estate, health	Regulatory complexity and operating bottlenecks	Structured FDI, SPVs, holding entities	Strong corridor familiarity but non-angel entry logic
Balkans–European diaspora	Opportunity-driven SMEs and export services	Intermediary gaps and variable ecosystem depth	Intermediated angel vehicles and diaspora-linked SME funds	Diaspora role depends on local absorptive capacity
African returnee corridors to West and East Africa	Trade-linked SMEs, services, and selected growth ventures	Institutional friction and uneven ecosystem depth	Selective angel syndicates or intermediary-led funds	Returnee investors respond to a mix of push and pull factors

Source Author's own elaboration based on Kontakos and Stavrou (2025), Mestwerdt et al. (2025), Mustafa (2021), Park and Tuxhorn (2025), Schmutzler et al. (2021), and related sources cited in the chapter

or blended funds rather than direct angel rounds. Sector fit, again, outruns broad national storytelling.

Once sectors are foregrounded, the dashboard becomes more precise and more honest. Investors stop asking whether a country is broadly attractive and start asking which combinations of sector, corridor, and vehicle can support disciplined returns.

Stage of finance also changes the meaning of sector fit. A corridor that works for seed-stage exportable software may be weak for growth-stage manufacturing if working-capital constraints, foreign-exchange exposure, or infrastructure deficits become binding later. Likewise, a corridor that is unattractive for pre-seed consumer ventures may still be a strong candidate for later-stage project development in energy, water, or logistics. Dashboards become more useful when they are updated by stage as well as by sector. The relevant question is not only where diaspora capital can enter, but whether the corridor can carry the company or project into its next financing threshold.

Sector concentration risk should be read alongside diaspora familiarity. Investors are often drawn to sectors they understand from their own migration or professional history, which can be beneficial up to a point. The danger is that familiarity narrows the opportunity set too much or leads investors to overlook sectors where diaspora advantage is weaker but market fundamentals are stronger. A sound dashboard keeps both questions visible. It asks where the diaspora edge exists and whether too much capital is already crowding into the same familiar segments.

A strong dashboard therefore checks whether diaspora advantage is likely to persist beyond entry (Yasin & Poulin, 2025; Yasin et al., 2025). Can the corridor still help at customer expansion, follow-on fundraising, regulatory navigation, or exit preparation? Or does the diaspora edge disappear after the first cheque? That distinction is crucial because some sectors are easy to source but hard to support over time. The best corridor–sector combinations are those in which diaspora value compounds across stages rather than peaking at introduction. Table 2 links sectors to diaspora advantages, potential misfits, and suitable investment instruments.

5 Using Dashboards Without Turning Them into Rankings

A country dashboard should guide decisions, not replace them. Its first use is screening. Investors can eliminate obvious mismatches early by asking whether the corridor has enough familiarity to interpret signals, enough institutional reliability to protect rights, enough sector depth to sustain pipeline quality, enough exit visibility to justify equity risk, and the right instrument fit for the opportunity at hand. That sequence is far more useful than a generic "diaspora-friendly" label.

Its second use is portfolio design. A diaspora investor or syndicate may decide that one corridor is suitable for direct angel rounds, another for SPV-based co-investment, and a third for larger project or thematic vehicles. This is where the comparative literature becomes especially valuable. India may support broader participation across venture stages because the entrepreneurial-finance ecosystem is deeper. South Africa–Europe may support highly selective angel syndicates with stronger diligence demands. Cyprus–Israel may be better approached through structured holding and FDI routes. Balkan corridors may reward intermediary-led ecosystem plays rather than atomized solo investing. A dashboard helps investors see these differences before capital is committed.

Its third use is policy discipline. Governments frequently try to mobilize diaspora capital through outreach campaigns, symbolic recognition, or patriotic language. Those tools may help at the margin, but the literature repeatedly shows that policy effectiveness depends on institutional follow-through (Brinkerhoff, 2012; Park, 2021;

Table 2 Sector–instrument fit across diaspora investment settings

Sector	Why diaspora advantage may matter	Where misfit often appears	Better vehicle choice
Exportable digital and B2B services	Market access, credibility, and customer introductions travel well	Overpricing based on global comparables alone	Angel syndicates or SPVs with strong follow-on networks
Healthcare and regulated services	Trust, institutional navigation, and professional networks matter	Licensing and compliance can delay scaling	Staged angel rounds with milestone finance
Climate and clean-tech ventures	Mission alignment can widen investor interest	Long timelines and project complexity exceed classic angel capacity	Blended vehicles or project-linked structures
Real estate, hospitality, and gateway services	Diaspora familiarity can support larger committed capital	Often treated as startup investing when the logic is closer to FDI	Structured FDI or holding-entity investment
Manufacturing and supply-chain ventures	Diaspora market access may help with buyers and suppliers	Working-capital and infrastructure demands can exceed angel capacity	Structured growth capital or blended vehicles
Consumer internet and local platforms	Diaspora branding may help early visibility	Exit dependence on domestic market depth is often high	Use very selective angel equity or avoid where exits are thin

Source Author's own elaboration based on Botelho et al. (2023), Dizo-Conteh et al. (2025), Kontakos and Stavrou (2025), and the wider corridor evidence discussed in the chapter

Ragazzi, 2014). A well-designed dashboard can show policymakers where the real bottlenecks sit. Sometimes the issue is not diasporic willingness. It is the absence of clean structures, sector-ready pipelines, or credible exit channels.

The final point is methodological. Dashboards should remain comparative, not absolute. They need updating as policy, macroeconomic conditions, and sector composition change. Used properly, they make diaspora investing more selective, less sentimental, and ultimately more scalable. Used badly, they become another ranking exercise that obscures the corridor-specific logic that actually drives outcomes.

For investors, one concrete benefit of this approach is portfolio coherence. Instead of accumulating homeland-adjacent deals opportunistically, a diaspora investor can decide in advance which corridors deserve direct angel exposure, which require syndication, which are better treated through funds or SPVs, and which should be reserved for larger thematic or project vehicles. That disciplined choice improves both risk management and founder support. It also makes cross-chapter tools in this volume more coherent, because valuation, syndication, and vehicle selection become functions of corridor fit rather than isolated techniques.

Dashboards also need to be revised after macro or policy shocks. Exchange-rate changes, capital-control adjustments, new investment incentives, conflict, visa policy, or a sudden increase in sector-specific acquirer interest can change corridor attractiveness much faster than diaspora narratives do. Investors who treat the dashboard as a living tool are better prepared to reallocate attention when those shifts occur. In that sense, the dashboard is not only a comparative framework. It is a discipline of updating assumptions before the next round or the next corridor expansion is priced.

There is a learning effect too. Once investors start comparing corridors systematically, they become better at noticing what made earlier deals work. They see when a strong local lead mattered more than diaspora identity, when a clean SPV outperformed a crowded cap table, or when sector choice overcame institutional weakness. Over time, the dashboard becomes less a static document and more a repository of investment memory. That is exactly what mature diaspora investing needs if it is to move from episodic enthusiasm to repeatable allocation discipline.

6 Conclusion

Country dashboards are valuable because they move diaspora investing away from generic enthusiasm and toward structured comparison. The evidence assembled here suggests that diaspora capital behaves differently across corridors not because identity stops mattering, but because identity interacts with institutions, sectors, and instruments in highly uneven ways.

For investors, the implication is practical. Compare corridors on familiarity, institutional reliability, sector depth, exit visibility, and vehicle fit before comparing them on narrative appeal. For policymakers, the lesson is equally direct. Mobilizing diaspora capital requires more than outreach. It requires corridors that are workable in commercial and legal terms. Where those conditions are present, diaspora capital can become a durable part of entrepreneurial finance. Where they are absent, good intentions will not close the gap.

Used in that spirit, a country dashboard is not a static scorecard. It is a living filter that helps investors and policymakers choose where diaspora capital can do its best work and where another form of capital is more appropriate. That is precisely the kind of maturity the field now needs: not a louder celebration of diaspora resources, but a sharper understanding of how, where, and through which channels those resources generate durable impact.

References

Botelho, T., Mason, C., & Chalvatzis, K. (2023). 50 shades of green—Angel investing in green businesses. *IEEE Transactions on Engineering Management, 70*(3), 950–962. https://doi.org/10.1109/TEM.2022.3167282

Brinkerhoff, J. M. (2012). Creating an enabling environment for diasporas' participation in homeland development. *International Migration, 50*(1), 75–95. https://doi.org/10.1111/j.1468-2435.2009.00542.x

Dizo-Conteh, U., Tasavori, M., & Afrahi, B. (2025). The contribution of diaspora networks to the internationalisation of SMEs: A case study in the healthcare industry. *Journal of International Management, 31*(6), Article 101306. https://doi.org/10.1016/j.intman.2025.101306

Kontakos, P., & Stavrou, S. (2025). Israeli and Jewish diaspora investment in Cyprus: FDI determinants, entry modes, and institutional challenges. *Journal of East-West Business*. Advance online publication. https://doi.org/10.1080/10669868.2025.2595351

Leblang, D. (2010). Familiarity breeds investment: Diaspora networks and international investment. *American Political Science Review, 104*(3), 584–600. https://doi.org/10.1017/S0003055410000201

Mestwerdt, S., Mrożewski, M., Sydow, A., & Burkert, N. (2025). Unveiling signaling processes in early-stage cross-border investment: Evidence from South African entrepreneurs and European business angels. *Journal of World Business, 60*(5), Article 101662. https://doi.org/10.1016/j.jwb.2025.101662

Mustafa, M. (2021). Angel investing: The untold story of India. *Palgrave Macmillan*. https://doi.org/10.1007/978-981-16-0921-3

Nyame-Asiamah, F., Amoako, I. O., Amankwah-Amoah, J., & Debrah, Y. A. (2020). Diaspora entrepreneurs' push and pull institutional factors for investing in Africa: Insights from African returnees from the United Kingdom. *Technological Forecasting and Social Change, 152*, Article 119876. https://doi.org/10.1016/j.techfore.2019.119876

Ojo, S., Nwankwo, S., & Gbadamosi, A. (2013). African diaspora entrepreneurs: Navigating entrepreneurial spaces in 'home' and 'host' countries. *International Journal of Entrepreneurship and Innovation, 14*(4), 289–299. https://doi.org/10.5367/ijei.2013.0126

Park, S. B. (2021). Courting foreign direct investment from diasporas: Are diaspora engagement policies effective? Under what conditions? *Pacific Focus, 36*(2), 252–286. https://doi.org/10.1111/pafo.12188

Park, S., & Tuxhorn, K.-L. (2025). Investment across borders: How diaspora firms weigh financial returns and emotional-social drivers. *Asian and Pacific Migration Journal, 34*(4), 653–675. https://doi.org/10.1177/01171968251393548

Ragazzi, F. (2014). A comparative analysis of diaspora policies. *Political Geography, 41*, 74–89. https://doi.org/10.1016/j.polgeo.2013.12.004

Ratha, D., Plaza, S., & Kim, E. J. (2024, December 18). In 2024, remittance flows to low- and middle-income countries are expected to reach $685 billion, larger than FDI and ODA combined. People Move. *World Bank Blogs*. https://blogs.worldbank.org/en/peoplemove/in-2024--remittance-flows-to-low--and-middle-income-countries-ar

Riddle, L., Hrivnak, G. A., & Nielsen, T. M. (2010). Transnational diaspora entrepreneurship in emerging markets: Bridging institutional divides. *Journal of International Management, 16*(4), 398–411. https://doi.org/10.1016/j.intman.2010.09.009

Schmutzler, J., Andonova, V., & Perez-Lopez, J. (2021). The role of diaspora in opportunity-driven entrepreneurial ecosystems: A mixed-methods study of Balkan economies. *International Entrepreneurship and Management Journal, 17*(2), 693–729. https://doi.org/10.1007/s11365-020-00708-4

Tong, S. Y. (2005). Ethnic networks in FDI and the impact of institutional development. *Review of Development Economics, 9*(4), 563–580. https://doi.org/10.1111/j.1467-9361.2005.00294.x

Ye, M. (2014). Diasporas and foreign direct investment in China and India. *Cambridge University Press*. https://doi.org/10.1017/CBO9781107286214

Yasin, N., and Hafeez, K. (2023). Three Waves of Immigrant Entrepreneurship. A Cross-National Comparative Study. *Small Business Economics: An Entrepreneurship Journal, 60*(1), 1281–1306

Yasin, N., Haq, M., Hafeez, K., & Zahoor, N. (2025). Are some immigrant entrepreneurs more privileged than others? A cross-national comparison of financial capital among start-ups in the

UK and UAE. *The Journal of Race, Ethnicity, and Politics*, 1–24. https://doi.org/10.1017/rep.2025.10031

Yasin, N., & Poulin, M. (2025). Developing a nation of entrepreneurs: The integral role of immigrant entrepreneurship for the United Arab Emirates Vision 2030. In C. Margaça, A. Walmsley & H. Knörr (Eds.), *Immigrant entrepreneurship, religion, and ethnicity: Cases from Europe, Africa, and Asia* (pp. 187–204). Routledge. https://doi.org/10.4324/9781003489214-12

Policy Incentives for Diaspora Angel Investing: Matching Funds, Tax Relief, and Co-Investment that Actually Travel

Matteo Rossi

Abstract This chapter examines how public policy can support diaspora angel investing without crowding out private judgment or mistaking symbolic outreach for market development. The focus is on mature instruments rather than speculative proposals. Synthesizing research on business angel policy, diaspora engagement, co-investment funds, and tax incentives, the chapter explains why public intervention is often justified in thin and cross-border early-stage markets and why many incentive schemes disappoint in practice. It shows that matching funds and co-investment vehicles can strengthen the financing chain by leveraging private selection and preserving commercial discipline. It also shows that tax relief can improve downside sharing, but only when rules are simple, credible, and aligned with actual investor behavior. The final section argues for a policy portfolio approach that combines capital instruments with data, regulation, standardized intermediation, and corridor-level infrastructure. The chapter offers a pragmatic guide to policies that help diaspora angel capital scale responsibly rather than rhetorically.

1 Introduction

Governments are strongly attracted to diaspora finance because it appears to promise three things at once: private capital, local commitment, and international reach. That appeal is understandable, but it often produces weak policy design. Too many interventions assume that investors are waiting only for a patriotic appeal or a small fiscal incentive. The evidence suggests otherwise. Diaspora angel investing grows when a policy ecosystem makes early-stage equity more investable, more legible, and less operationally fragile across borders (Brinkerhoff, 2012; Park, 2021; Ragazzi, 2014).

This matters because cross-border angel investing faces a particular form of market failure. Search costs are high, verification is expensive, small-ticket deals struggle to bear legal and due diligence overheads, and early investors create spillovers that later financiers can exploit. Those conditions can justify public support. They do not

M. Rossi (✉)
University of Sannio, Benevento, Italy
e-mail: mrossi@unisannio.it

H. Jarrar et al. (eds.), *Diaspora Angel Investing*, Ethnic and Indigenous Business Studies, https://doi.org/10.1007/978-3-032-33088-8_9

justify replacing private judgment. The policy challenge is to lower frictions without socializing selection in a way that weakens screening discipline (Harrison, 2022; Harrison et al., 2020; Mason et al., 2022).

In practice, three families of instruments dominate the discussion. Matching funds seek to multiply private angel capital in targeted deals. Tax relief aims to improve the risk-return profile of early-stage investing. Co-investment mechanisms create structured ways for public money to follow, rather than precede, credible private investors. Each can work. Each can also fail when it is designed as a gesture rather than as part of a financing chain.

This chapter reviews those instruments with a specific diaspora lens. The question is not how states can celebrate diasporas. The question is how they can help diaspora angels invest with commercial discipline in markets where distance, fragmentation, and weak intermediation otherwise block deal formation.

That distinction is particularly important for diaspora investing because policy-makers often confuse willingness to engage with willingness to invest. Diaspora professionals may be happy to mentor, advise, donate, or join symbolic initiatives while still declining equity deals they cannot diligence or exit with confidence. Public policy, therefore, fails when it assumes that patriotic intent can substitute for an investable market. Mature evidence points the other way. Investors respond when frictions around sourcing, verification, structuring, and follow-on finance are reduced in concrete ways rather than narrated away (Brinkerhoff, 2012; Park, 2021; Ragazzi, 2014).

A second complication is that diaspora angel markets are corridor specific. The relevant bottlenecks differ sharply depending on tax treaties, foreign exchange rules, sanctions screening, company law, and the presence or absence of credible local lead investors. This means that incentive design should not begin with a generic global template. It should begin with a map of where deals are already almost investable and where a targeted public intervention could move them from episodic to repeatable. The most useful policies amplify private discovery already underway instead of trying to create investor confidence through announcement effects alone.

2 Why Policy Support is Justified but Must Remain Disciplined

The strongest case for intervention begins with the nature of the early-stage equity gap. Young firms that are too risky for banks and too small for institutional venture funds often depend on angels for their first credible external equity. In cross-border settings, that gap is magnified by travel costs, legal complexity, limited local bias-reduction mechanisms, and weaker visibility into deal flow. These are not problems that private investors can always solve efficiently on their own, especially when the market is still forming (Cumming & Zhang, 2019; Harrison et al., 2020; Mason et al., 2022; Yasin and Hafeez, 2023).

Public support is therefore defensible when it addresses genuine coordination failures. A government can help make the market more legible by supporting standardized documents, trusted investor networks, regulatory clarity, and market data. It can also help deals become larger and more financeable by matching private rounds or creating co-investment vehicles that sit alongside experienced angels. The critical design issue is whether the intervention strengthens or weakens private selection (Harrison, 2022).

That distinction matters even more in diaspora settings. Diaspora capital is sometimes treated as if identity reduces risk. It does not. It changes the information structure. Policy should therefore focus on making cross-border diligence, enforcement, and syndication easier rather than assuming that cultural affinity alone will unlock scalable capital. The broader diaspora policy literature is clear that mobilization works best when enabling conditions are real rather than performative (Brinkerhoff, 2012; Park, 2021; Ragazzi, 2014).

This is also why purely symbolic incentives tend to disappoint. Investor decisions are shaped by pipeline quality, trust in institutions, tax clarity, expected returns, and realistic exit pathways. Outreach campaigns may improve awareness. They rarely alter those fundamentals. The most effective policies usually operate closer to the actual bottlenecks of the deal process: origination, verification, legal execution, syndication, and follow-on funding (Harrison, 2022; Mason et al., 2022).

A disciplined policy stance, therefore, begins with humility. Governments do not need to pick the best founders. They need to improve the conditions under which capable private investors can find, assess, and support those founders across borders.

The market failure case is strongest where early-stage equity generates spillovers that private actors cannot fully capture. A lead angel who spends time educating founders, cleaning the cap table, and establishing reporting discipline may create value that later investors can benefit from without incurring the original search and monitoring costs. In cross-border settings, those frictions are multiplied by travel, legal translation, and coordination across advisors. Public support is therefore easier to justify when it lowers the cost of activities that improve the market as a whole, such as network formation, standard documentation, or co-investment alongside credible private leads.

Even so, additionality is the central test. A policy that merely subsidizes investments that would have occurred anyway is expensive public relations, not market-building. That is why the angel policy literature is skeptical of indiscriminate subsidy. The relevant question is whether the instrument attracts more investors, larger rounds, or stronger follow-on outcomes than the market would have produced unaided. If it does not, public money is simply replacing private capital or rewarding activity after the fact (Carpentier & Suret, 2007, 2016; Harrison, 2022; Harrison et al., 2020).

Diaspora settings make this discipline even more necessary because identity can create political pressure to support visible deals. Yet visibility and additionality are not the same. A highly publicized diaspora round may still be a weak policy target if it relies on a single charismatic founder, a single symbolic event, or a one-off patriotic mobilization. Better public interventions help many deals become more executable, not one deal become more celebrated.

3 Matching Funds and Co-Investment Work Best When They Follow Private Judgment

Matching funds and co-investment vehicles are attractive because they can increase round size without forcing the state to become the primary selector of ventures. In principle, this aligns public support with the discovery function that angels perform. In practice, design details are decisive. If public money enters only after experienced investors have completed screening and committed capital on commercial terms, the instrument can deepen the market while preserving discipline. If public money drives the process, the selection signal weakens, and the market may become more political than investable (Harrison, 2022; Harrison et al., 2020).

The United Kingdom's Angel CoFund experience is instructive in this respect. Early assessments suggest that co-investment can improve access to finance for ventures that require larger early rounds, especially when the market struggles to provide sufficient patient equity at the right stage. At the same time, the benefits depend on strong private lead investors and careful governance. Co-investment is most effective when it complements syndicates that already know how to screen, negotiate, and monitor rather than trying to create those capabilities from scratch (Owen & Mason, 2017).

The more recent Regional Angels Programme extends that logic by explicitly seeking to unlock additional private capital and reduce regional imbalances in access to early-stage equity. What makes this relevant for diaspora investing is not only the public money itself. It is the recognition that the market needs structured partners, local knowledge, and co-investment pathways if smaller and geographically dispersed deals are to become financeable at scale (British Business Bank, n.d.).

For diaspora corridors, matching mechanisms are especially useful when deals are credible but too small or too complicated to attract purely domestic syndicates. A well-designed public match can help a diaspora angel round reach the size needed for proper governance, legal work, and follow-on preparedness. Yet the public component should remain catalytic. Once the state becomes the reason a deal exists, rather than the reason it reaches efficient scale, the instrument usually begins to distort selection.

Pricing discipline is crucial here. Public money should not quietly encourage overvaluation by allowing rounds to clear at terms that private investors would not otherwise accept. If the state is going to match, it should usually do so on the same commercial terms as the lead private investors and with governance rights that avoid crowding the cap table. This preserves a clean signal for future financiers. It also keeps founders from receiving a distorted message about what the market is actually willing to bear.

The mature lesson is that co-investment should behave like disciplined leverage. It should enlarge the market discovered by private angels, not simulate one that does not yet exist.

This is why lead investor quality sits at the center of good co-investment design. Public money should usually follow an investor or syndicate that can demonstrate sector understanding, relevant due diligence, and a credible willingness to monitor the company after closing. The objective is not simply to reduce risk through shared funding. It is to keep the discovery function in private hands while giving promising companies access to rounds that are large enough to support proper governance and early scaling. The evidence from co-investment schemes suggests that governance quality, not just capital quantity, explains much of the difference between catalytic and distortive programs (Harrison et al., 2020; Owen & Mason, 2017).

For diaspora corridors, the matching design should also account for the reality of small-ticket fragmentation. A deal that looks modest in a mature ecosystem may be transformative in a thinner market, yet still too small to absorb the fixed cost of legal work and monitoring. A well-calibrated match can solve that problem by making the round big enough to justify disciplined execution. But the calibration matters. Ratios that are too generous weaken price discovery, while ratios that are too small leave the underlying coordination problem untouched. A catalytic scheme usually matches enough to improve viability while preserving private investor exposure to downside.

Another lesson from organized angel markets is that co-investment works better when embedded in functioning investor networks rather than as a stand-alone bureaucracy. Networks help identify credible leads, spread diligence effort, and build a pipeline of future investors. This matters for diaspora investing because many cross-border deals suffer less from absolute scarcity of money than from scarcity of organized intermediation. If policymakers want more diaspora angel activity, they often need to back the connective tissue around the deal as much as the capital inside it (Lahti & Keinonen, 2016; Mason et al., 2022). Table 1 compares the major policy instruments, the problems they address, and the design rules needed to avoid common failures.

Another design principle is to think in portfolio rather than project terms. A scheme can tolerate some company failures if it improves the overall quality, size, and continuity of the early-stage market. What it cannot tolerate is a pattern of deals that require subsidy to close but never become attractive to follow-on capital. That is why program managers should monitor not only whether money was deployed, but whether co-invested firms go on to raise again, professionalize governance, and expand the base of credible private investors around them.

This portfolio view is especially relevant for diaspora investing because governments may be tempted to judge success by the symbolism of a few highly visible homeland-linked deals. Yet a market deepens only when investors can repeat the process across multiple ventures without exceptional handholding. Good policy, therefore, rewards repeatability. It asks whether the instrument helped create more lead investors, more financeable founders, and more investable rounds in the corridor as a whole.

The instruments in the table should therefore be read as complements rather than substitutes (Yasin et al., 2025). A matching fund is far more effective when investor networks already exist and when tax treatment does not make cross-border participation cumbersome. Likewise, tax relief is more likely to mobilize new capital when investors can see a route into credible syndicated deals rather than facing

Table 1 How major policy instruments support diaspora angel markets and where they often fail

Instrument	Problem addressed	Frequent failure	Design rule
Matching funds	Rounds are too small to support proper governance and early scale	Public money leads instead of leveraging private selection	Match only after credible private investors commit on commercial terms
Co investment funds	Need for larger early rounds and risk sharing in thin markets	Weak lead investors and diffuse accountability	Use strong lead investor requirements and clear governance rights
Tax relief	Poor downside profile for high risk early stage investing	Rules are complex, unstable, or hard to interpret	Favor simple eligibility criteria, predictable administration, and policy continuity
Angel network support	Search, diligence, and syndication costs are high	Networks become symbolic clubs rather than screening platforms	Tie support to professional intermediation, data, and active deal management
Diaspora engagement initiatives	Investors lack corridor information and trusted entry points	Patriotic messaging substitutes for market reform	Link outreach to real legal, tax, and diligence infrastructure
Tax relief	Improves downside economics for risky early stage equity	Complex eligibility and compliance rules reduce take up and distort selection	Keep qualification rules stable, published, and easy for cross border investors and issuers to understand
Investor network support	Reduces search, diligence, and syndication frictions	Policy chases visibility rather than lead investor capability	Support investor groups, standard documents, and lead investor development rather than one off events
Corridor infrastructure	Addresses tax, legal, and compliance frictions specific to home host pathways	Generic national programs ignore the real bottlenecks that stop deals	Map high traffic corridors and fix the most costly execution barriers first
Data and evaluation	Shows whether schemes add capital, quality, and geographic spread	No evidence on additionality, follow on funding, or firm survival	Track deal size, investor mix, follow on rounds, and regional distribution from the start

Source Author's own elaboration based on Carpentier and Suret (2007, 2016), Harrison et al. (2020), Harrison (2022), Owen and Mason (2017), and Solodoha et al. (2023)

atomized, high-friction transactions. Mature policy design works on the financing chain, not on one isolated policy lever.

Mis-sequencing is one of the most common policy errors. Governments often launch a visible fiscal incentive before building the quieter infrastructure that makes investors comfortable using it. When legal templates are weak, lead investors are scarce, and local advisors are unfamiliar with early-stage equity, the incentive may generate noise but not disciplined deployment. In such cases, the first public money may be better spent on market organization and capability building than on a headline subsidy.

This is also where corridor mapping becomes useful. Diaspora capital rarely arrives from everywhere at once. It clusters in pathways where migration history, sector specialization, or professional associations already create a base layer of familiarity. Public agencies that identify those corridors can design more intelligent support, for example, by clarifying tax treatment for nonresident investors, simplifying onboarding for compliance, or supporting investor forums tied to real-sector opportunities rather than generic promotional events.

4 Tax Relief Can Help, but Only if the Design is Simple and Credible

Tax relief remains one of the most common angel policy tools because it changes the downside profile of risky early-stage investments. In theory, that can draw more private investors into the market and encourage them to back younger firms. The empirical and policy literature, however, is more cautious than the popularity of these schemes suggests. Relief matters, but it is rarely sufficient on its own. Investors respond not only to generosity but also to clarity, administrative burden, confidence in eligibility, and whether the broader market offers plausible follow-on and exit paths (Carpentier & Suret, 2007, 2016).

This is why simple schemes often outperform clever ones. When investors cannot predict whether a company will qualify, whether documentation will be accepted, or whether subsequent changes in status will result in clawbacks of benefits, the tax incentive loses its force. Worse, ambiguity can change investor behavior in unintended ways. Evidence from Israel shows that a policy designed to encourage angel investment can reduce the number of angels per targeted startup when investors perceive ambiguity or added compliance risk. The incentive exists on paper, yet its design raises caution rather than confidence (Solodoha et al., 2023).

The United Kingdom remains the best-known contemporary example of tax-supported early-stage equity through the Enterprise Investment Scheme and the Seed Enterprise Investment Scheme. The policy significance of these instruments lies not only in the relief they provide but also in their embeddedness in the wider market infrastructure. Statistics and guidance are transparent; investors understand the categories reasonably well; and the schemes are part of a broader financing environment rather than a standalone gesture (HM Revenue & Customs, 2025).

For diaspora investors, the lesson is not that every country should replicate the British model word for word. The real lesson is design integrity. Relief should be intelligible to cross-border investors, compatible with local corporate law, and supported by guidance that reduces uncertainty rather than multiplying it. Broad comparative reviews of tax incentives for venture capital and angels show that countries use many variants, but good practice repeatedly points toward clarity, stability, and integration with other policy tools rather than isolated fiscal generosity (European Commission, 2017).

Tax relief, then, should be treated as one piece of a broader risk-sharing architecture. It can enhance the appeal of early-stage investing, but it cannot compensate for weak diligence channels, unreliable enforcement, or a lack of quality deal flow.

Tax design becomes even more delicate when nonresident or diaspora investors are involved. Relief that works well for resident taxpayers may be unusable across borders if eligibility depends on domestic tax status, if treaty treatment is unclear, or if documentation requirements are difficult to satisfy from abroad. Governments sometimes announce broad openness to diaspora investment while quietly leaving these practical questions unresolved. The result is an incentive that exists on paper but fails in the transaction. Good design, therefore, asks not only whether the relief is generous, but whether the intended investor can actually claim it without disproportionate legal cost.

Administrative stability matters as much as headline generosity. Investors planning multi-year portfolios pay attention to whether schemes are politically durable, whether guidance is updated clearly, and whether the treatment of follow-on rounds or holding periods is predictable. Evidence from comparative reviews and natural experiments suggests that incentives can influence behavior, but only when the rule set is credible, and the compliance burden does not overwhelm the benefit. Poorly specified tax relief can even create unintended concentration, encouraging investors to optimize for eligibility rather than for venture quality (Carpentier & Suret, 2007, 2016; Solodoha et al., 2023).

The British experience is instructive precisely because it shows tax relief embedded in a broader ecosystem rather than operating in isolation. Public statistics, established intermediaries, standard market knowledge, and complementary co-investment channels all make the scheme more legible to investors. The transferable lesson is not that every country should copy the exact percentages. It is that relief works best when it forms part of an understandable financing system rather than a technically generous but administratively mysterious instrument (European Commission, 2017; HM Revenue & Customs, 2025; Yasin & Poulin, 2025).

Cross-border usability should also be tested explicitly. Can a diaspora investor understand the treatment of dividends, capital gains, withholding, and loss relief without hiring a team of specialist advisors? Can the company explain eligibility confidently to a nonresident lead investor? Are there administrative procedures that routinely delay closing or create uncertainty around qualification? These questions sound technical, but they often determine whether an incentive influences real behavior or remains largely rhetorical.

5 The Right Policy Portfolio is Wider Than Capital Instruments Alone

A mature diaspora angel policy does not begin and end with money. It also requires the institutions that make private selection credible. Investor networks, standardized term sheets, data rooms, legal onboarding support, clarity on dispute resolution, and reliable investment statistics all matter because they reduce the transaction costs of investing small amounts across borders. Research on business angel networks shows that organized intermediation can improve access to deals and spread evaluation capabilities, which is especially valuable when investors are dispersed across countries (Lahti & Keinonen, 2016).

Corridor-specific infrastructure matters as well. Diaspora investment rarely happens in the abstract. It happens between particular home and host countries with specific migration histories, tax relationships, compliance burdens, and industry strengths. A policy that ignores those corridor realities tends to produce generic slogans rather than functioning channels. Better policy identifies where diaspora investors already possess useful commercial reach and then reduces the frictions that stop them from acting professionally at scale (Brinkerhoff, 2012; Park, 2021).

There is also a sequencing issue. In very early ecosystems, it may be wiser to fund network formation, lead investor capability, and standardization before launching ambitious fiscal incentives. In more developed ecosystems, matching and co-investment can strengthen the financing escalator by helping angel-backed firms reach a size that later investors can support. The policy portfolio should therefore adapt to market maturity rather than remain fixed by ideology (Harrison, 2022; Owen & Mason, 2017).

Most importantly, the state should resist the temptation to turn diaspora investing into a test of loyalty. Commercially serious diaspora investors want functioning markets, not ceremonial recognition alone. They respond to credible institutions, predictable treatment, and investable pipelines. Policies that frame them primarily as patriotic financiers may generate visibility, but they rarely build repeatable early-stage markets (Park, 2021; Ragazzi, 2014).

The strongest policy ecosystem is therefore modular. It combines targeted capital instruments with trustworthy intermediation, intelligible tax design, corridor-aware regulation, and enough public data for investors to judge whether the market is improving. That is the route by which diaspora angel investing becomes durable rather than episodic.

A second practical issue is the credibility of implementation. Investors pay close attention to whether agencies answer questions consistently, process approvals on time, and communicate changes to program rules clearly. A theoretically sound scheme can underperform badly if administrative friction remains high. This is especially true for diaspora investors who are comparing the burden of one corridor with opportunities elsewhere. In effect, implementation quality becomes part of the market signal.

Evaluation should also focus on whether public schemes improve the quality of capital, not only the quantity. A larger number of subsidized deals is not enough if rounds remain undersized, follow-on rates stay weak, or founder governance does not improve. Strong evaluation asks whether the program helped ventures attract better syndicates, achieve longer investment horizons, and progress more cleanly to the next financing stage. Those outcomes indicate market deepening rather than temporary stimulation.

Over time, the most credible states will likely be the ones that learn publicly. They will publish deal statistics, acknowledge where instruments are underperforming, and revise schemes without pretending that every diaspora initiative is automatically strategic. That posture matters because it signals seriousness to investors. It tells them that the government understands early-stage finance as a learning process rather than as a branding exercise.

This is why noncapital infrastructure deserves more policy attention than it often receives. Standard term sheets, template shareholder agreements, model data room checklists, guidance on foreign investor onboarding, and clarity on dispute resolution may appear mundane compared with a matching fund announcement, but they often have a greater impact on transaction feasibility. They reduce the fixed cost of doing small cross-border deals and make syndication easier because everyone is working from more legible documents and expectations.

Skills policy also belongs in this conversation. A diaspora angel market deepens when founders understand investor reporting, when lawyers and accountants can competently handle early-stage equity, and when local accelerators know how to prepare companies for external due diligence. Public agencies do not need to deliver all of that directly, but they can support the intermediaries that do. In immature ecosystems, capability building may yield more additionality than a generous fiscal incentive launched into a pipeline that is not yet finance ready.

Finally, policy should be evaluated corridor by corridor and stage by stage. A program may work well for software founders connecting London and Lagos, poorly for deep manufacturing ventures with long asset cycles, and differently again for returnee investors in Balkan or Mediterranean pathways. Mature policy learning does not hide this heterogeneity. It measures it. That allows governments to refine instruments, retire weak schemes, and channel scarce fiscal effort toward the points in the market where catalytic effects are genuinely plausible.

Sequencing matters here as well. In nascent markets, the best public spending may be on legal clarity, investor education, founder readiness, and organized syndication. In intermediate markets, matching and co-investment may become more effective because there is already enough private capability to select and monitor deals. In stronger markets, the policy problem may shift again toward regional inclusion, scale-up finance, or the internationalization of investor networks. Treating every ecosystem as if it needed the same instrument at the same time is one of the fastest ways to waste scarce public resources.

6 Conclusion

Public policy can play a legitimate role in diaspora angel investing because the underlying market suffers from real frictions. Small deal sizes, distance, weak intermediation, and costly verification all slow the movement of equity into promising ventures. Matching funds, co-investment vehicles, and tax relief can help. Yet the evidence also makes a harder point. These instruments work only when they reinforce private judgment rather than attempting to replace it.

For that reason, the best diaspora angel policy is never a single instrument. It is a portfolio that combines catalytic capital with trustworthy rules, functioning intermediaries, and corridor-specific infrastructure. When those pieces line up, public support does not artificially manufacture a market. It helps a real market become investable at scale. That is the standard policymakers should aim for if they want diaspora capital to become a durable part of entrepreneurial finance rather than a recurring slogan.

The practical implication is straightforward. Governments should resist designing diaspora angel policy as a symbolic invitation and instead treat it as a problem of market engineering. The question is never whether diaspora investors care. The question is whether the rules, intermediaries, and incentives allow that interest to turn into disciplined, repeat investment. When they do, public support can be catalytic. When they do not, even generous schemes will struggle to move beyond isolated success stories.

This also means that the benchmark for success should be stricter than political visibility. A good diaspora angel policy should make it easier for serious investors to transact repeatedly, not just easier for governments to announce that they welcome investment. The relevant evidence is whether more ventures receive properly structured rounds, whether lead investors become stronger, whether follow-on capital becomes easier to attract, and whether corridor frictions fall in ways that investors can actually feel.

Countries that get this right are likely to look less theatrical and more administratively competent. Their incentives will be published clearly, their co-investment processes will be intelligible, their investor networks will be connected to real deal flow, and their public agencies will learn from data rather than from anecdote. That kind of credibility matters because diaspora investors constantly compare jurisdictions. They notice where rules are stable, where legal execution is predictable, and where public partners understand the economics of small high-risk deals.

In that sense, the most successful policy package is one that eventually becomes almost unremarkable to use. It does not force investors to navigate patriotic theater or bureaucratic improvisation. It simply reduces the friction of doing sensible cross-border early-stage deals. When policy reaches that level of usability, diaspora angel capital can move from episodic mobilization to a durable place within the entrepreneurial finance system.

References

British Business Bank. (n.d.). Regional angels programme. https://www.british-business-bank.co.uk/finance-options/equity-finance/regional-angels-programme

Brinkerhoff, J. M. (2012). Creating an enabling environment for diasporas' participation in homeland development. *International Migration, 50*(1), 75–95. https://doi.org/10.1111/j.1468-2435.2009.00542.x

Carpentier, C., & Suret, J.-M. (2007). On the usefulness of tax incentives for informal investors. *Venture Capital, 9*(1), 1–22. https://doi.org/10.1080/13691060600996673

Carpentier, C., & Suret, J.-M. (2016). The effectiveness of tax incentives for business angels. In H. Landström & C. Mason (Eds.), *Handbook of research on business angels* (pp. 327–353). Edward Elgar Publishing. https://doi.org/10.4337/9781783471720.00021

Cumming, D., & Zhang, M. (2019). Angel investors around the world. *Journal of International Business Studies, 50*(5), 692–719. https://doi.org/10.1057/s41267-018-0178-0

European Commission. (2017). Effectiveness of tax incentives for venture capital and business angels to foster the investment of SMEs and start-ups. https://taxation-customs.ec.europa.eu/system/files/2017-06/final_report_2017_taxud_venture-capital_business-angels.pdf

Harrison, R. T. (2022). "Pennies from heaven"? Market failure, circuits of capital and policy support for business angels: The case of cross-border angel investment. *Journal of Business Venturing Insights, 17*, Article e00311. https://doi.org/10.1016/j.jbvi.2022.e00311

Harrison, R. T., Bock, A. J., & Gregson, G. (2020). Stairway to heaven? Rethinking angel investment policy and practice. *Journal of Business Venturing Insights, 14*, Article e00180. https://doi.org/10.1016/j.jbvi.2020.e00180

HM Revenue & Customs. (2025, May 14). Enterprise investment scheme, seed enterprise investment scheme and social investment tax relief statistics 2025. https://www.gov.uk/government/statistics/enterprise-investment-scheme-seed-enterprise-investment-scheme-and-social-investment-tax-relief-may-2025/enterprise-investment-scheme-seed-enterprise-investment-scheme-and-social-investment-tax-relief-statistics-2025

Lahti, T., & Keinonen, H. (2016). Business angel networks: A review and assessment of their value to entrepreneurship. In H. Landström & C. Mason (Eds.), Handbook of research on business angels (pp. 354–378). Edward Elgar Publishing. https://doi.org/10.4337/9781783471720.00022

Mason, C., Botelho, T., & Duggett, J. (2022). Promoting cross-border investing by business angels in the European Union. *Regional Studies, 56*(8), 1391–1403. https://doi.org/10.1080/00343404.2021.1960961

Owen, R., & Mason, C. (2017). The role of government co-investment funds in the supply of entrepreneurial finance: An assessment of the early operation of the UK Angel Co-investment fund. *Environment and Planning c: Politics and Space, 35*(3), 434–456. https://doi.org/10.1177/0263774X16667072

Park, S. B. (2021). Courting foreign direct investment from diasporas: Are diaspora engagement policies effective? Under what conditions? *Pacific Focus, 36*(2), 252–286. https://doi.org/10.1111/pafo.12188

Ragazzi, F. (2014). A comparative analysis of diaspora policies. *Political Geography, 41*, 74–89. https://doi.org/10.1016/j.polgeo.2013.12.004

Solodoha, E., Rosenzweig, S., & Harel, S. (2023). Incentivizing angels to invest in start-ups: Evidence from a natural experiment. *Research Policy, 52*(1), Article 104634. https://doi.org/10.1016/j.respol.2022.104634

Yasin, N., Haq, M., Hafeez, K., & Zahoor, N. (2025). Are some immigrant entrepreneurs more privileged than others? A cross-national comparison of financial capital among start-ups in the UK and UAE. *The Journal of Race, Ethnicity, and Politics*, 1–24. https://doi.org/10.1017/rep.2025.10031

Yasin, N., & Hafeez, K. (2023). Three waves of immigrant entrepreneurship. A cross-national comparative study. *Small Business Economics: An Entrepreneurship Journal. 60*(1) pp.1281–1306 https://doi.org/10.1007/s11187-022-0065z

Yasin, N., & Poulin, M. (2025). Developing a nation of entrepreneurs: The integral role of immigrant entrepreneurship for the United Arab Emirates Vision 2030. In C. Margaça, A. Walmsley & H. Knörr (Eds.), *Immigrant entrepreneurship, religion, and ethnicity: Cases from Europe, Africa, and Asia* (pp. 187–204). Routledge. https://doi.org/10.4324/9781003489214-12

Diaspora Angel Investing in Transnational Entrepreneurial Finance: A Systematic and Bibliometric Review

Guido Migliaccio

Abstract This chapter examines diaspora angel investing within the domain of transnational entrepreneurial finance through a combined bibliometric and literature review. Drawing on a Scopus-based dataset and analyses conducted using VOSviewer, the study maps the intellectual, relational, and thematic structure of the field. The findings reveal a fragmented and weakly integrated body of literature, largely dominated by approaches centred on social capital, human capital, and migrant entrepreneurship. While these perspectives effectively explain the mobilization of diaspora resources, they offer limited insight into the financial structuring of investments. Investor-side dimensions, such as deal-sourcing, valuation, governance, and investment vehicles, remain marginal. This reveals a structural gap between relational foundations and the operational mechanisms required to scale investments. The chapter contributes to the volume by systematizing an emerging field and advancing a research agenda focused on financial models, contractual instruments, and scalable investment practices.

1 Introduction

The growing interest in the economic role of diasporas highlights how transnational networks, social capital, and international mobility contribute to the creation of new entrepreneurial ventures (Yasin & Hafeez, 2023). However, the literature has developed predominantly along sociological and entrepreneurial lines, emphasizing the role of networks in overcoming institutional and informational constraints (Riddle et al., 2010; Yasin, 2022). As a consequence, the financial dimension of the phenomenon, and in particular diaspora angel investing, remain underdeveloped. To understand this misalignment, it is necessary to examine the main existing theoretical strands. While prior studies provide robust evidence on the role of human and

G. Migliaccio (✉)
Department of Law, Economics, Management and Quantitative Methods (DEMM), University of Sannio, Benevento, Italy
e-mail: guido.migliaccio@unisannio.it

H. Jarrar et al. (eds.), *Diaspora Angel Investing*, Ethnic and Indigenous Business Studies, https://doi.org/10.1007/978-3-032-33088-8_10

social capital (Ma et al., 2019; Tolciu, 2011; Yasin et al., 2025), they still fail to offer analytical tools and operational models consistent with these requirements. There is therefore a clear need to develop investor-side approaches, focused on the operational mechanisms through which diaspora capital is mobilized, including deal-sourcing, trust, financial vehicles, valuation, and ESG criteria. This chapter addresses this gap through a systematic and bibliometric review, aimed at reconstructing the structure of the field and identifying its main research streams.

The integration of bibliometric analysis and systematic review mitigates the fragmentation of the literature, combining quantitative mapping with theoretical interpretation (Dabić et al., 2020). In line with established approaches, the proposed methodology enables the identification of thematic clusters, evolutionary trajectories, and research gaps, thereby providing an empirical basis for the development of a more coherent framework (Chhabra et al., 2022; Kumar et al., 2021).

The contribution of the chapter is twofold. On the one hand, it offers a structured synthesis of the literature on diaspora and transnational entrepreneurship, highlighting its interdisciplinary and fragmented nature. On the other hand, it identifies a misalignment between the capacity to mobilize capital and the ability to structure investments, advancing a research agenda oriented toward the development of financial models, contractual instruments, and operational practices consistent with the needs of the diaspora investor ecosystem.

2 Literature Review

The literature on diaspora angel investing lies at the intersection of diaspora entrepreneurship, transnational entrepreneurship, migrant entrepreneurship, and entrepreneurial finance. Foundational contributions within transnational entrepreneurship highlight how migrant entrepreneurs operate across multiple institutional contexts, mobilizing social, cognitive, and economic resources beyond national boundaries (Drori et al., 2009; Riddle et al., 2010). From this perspective, the diaspora is not merely an identity-based community, but an economic infrastructure capable of transferring knowledge, reputational capital, and market access, thereby contributing to the reduction of institutional gaps between home and host contexts (Kotabe et al., 2013; Riddle et al., 2010; Saxenian, 2005).

A first stream of research conceptualizes the diaspora through social capital, trust, and embeddedness. Diaspora networks reduce informational asymmetries, facilitate access to resources, and support the identification of entrepreneurial opportunities (Asante, 2018; Karayianni et al., 2023; Tolciu, 2011; Williams & Krasniqi, 2018). However, these studies tend to privilege the socio-relational dimension over the financial structure of investment. Social capital explains the conditions under which diaspora capital is mobilized, but not the mechanisms governing its allocation, valuation, and governance. This limitation represents the primary fault line between the existing literature and the investor-side perspective.

A second stream focuses on human capital, knowledge, and entrepreneurial return. Studies on returnee entrepreneurs show that international experience, technical competences, and transnational networks can enhance performance, legitimacy, and access to venture capital (Fuller, 2010; Ma et al., 2019; Wu & Ma, 2018). Similarly, the literature on brain circulation highlights how highly skilled communities can connect geographically distant innovation ecosystems, facilitating knowledge transfer and technological upgrading across national contexts (Saxenian, 2005). Yet, even in this case, the analytical focus remains primarily on the entrepreneur's profile rather than on investor decision-making.

A third, more recent stream links migration, digital finance, and access to funding. In emerging contexts, digital finance can mitigate informational and financial constraints that disadvantage migrant and returnee entrepreneurs, thereby expanding access to credit, capital, and entrepreneurial opportunities (Li et al., 2022; Liu et al., 2022; Yasin et al., 2024). This stream is particularly relevant as it moves the debate closer to the investor-side dimension. Nevertheless, it remains distant from the core instruments of angel investing, including syndication, Special Purpose Vehicles (SPVs), term sheets, valuation practices, exit strategies, and Environmental, Social and Governance (ESG) criteria.

Bibliometric and systematic reviews confirm the fragmentation of adjacent research domains. Studies on SME internationalization demonstrate the value of integrating bibliometric techniques with systematic review approaches in order to identify theoretical trajectories, methodological patterns, and cumulative research gaps (Dabić et al., 2020). Reviews in entrepreneurship and small business research further highlight the centrality of social capital, internationalization, minority entrepreneurship, and co-authorship in shaping the evolution of the field (Chhabra et al., 2022; Kumar et al., 2021). These contributions support the methodological design of this chapter and reinforce the need to treat diaspora angel investing as an emerging field, still lacking a consolidated theoretical structure.

The core gap is therefore clear. The literature provides robust explanations of networks, trust, human capital, and transnational embeddedness, yet it does not develop investor-side models capable of mobilizing diaspora capital at scale. There is a need to investigate operational instruments such as deal-sourcing mechanisms, trust-based due diligence, investment vehicles, valuation benchmarks, and ESG screening practices. This leads to the following research questions:

RQ1. What is the intellectual and relational structure of the literature on diaspora, transnational entrepreneurship, and entrepreneurial finance?

RQ2. Which thematic areas dominate the field, and which remain marginal from an investor-side perspective?

RQ3. To what extent does the existing literature provide theoretical and operational foundations for the development of diaspora angel investing as a distinct domain within entrepreneurial finance?

3 Methodology

This study adopts a systematic literature review integrated with bibliometric analysis, consistent with established methodological standards in management research (Donthu et al., 2021; Haq & Yasin, 2025; Zupic & Čater, 2015). The analysis identifies the thematic and relational structure of the field through a dataset constructed from Scopus, selected for its breadth, editorial quality, and widespread use in bibliometric studies (Donthu et al., 2021). The search query combines terms related to diaspora, investment, and entrepreneurship, and is applied to titles, abstracts, and keywords.

The search was conducted in May 2026. Studies examining the role of the diaspora in entrepreneurial finance processes are included, whereas contributions addressing migration or finance without reference to entrepreneurial activity are excluded. The analytical protocol follows established systematic review procedures (Tranfield et al., 2003).

Beyond the results provided by Scopus, the dataset is further analysed using VOSviewer, which enables the construction of bibliometric networks based on measurable relationships (Van Eck & Waltman, 2010, 2014). In line with the structure of the results, the analysis considers documents, authors, and their interrelations, and is articulated through bibliographic coupling, co-authorship, and keyword co-occurrence. Bibliographic coupling captures thematic proximity between studies based on shared references, co-authorship identifies collaborative networks among scholars, and co-occurrence analysis reveals conceptual structures through the frequency with which keywords appear jointly.

The resulting maps are network representations in which nodes correspond to units of analysis, namely documents, authors, and keywords, and their size reflects weight, measured by citations or occurrences. Connections indicate the existence of relationships, their thickness reflects intensity, spatial distance signals relational proximity, and colors identify relatively cohesive thematic clusters over time. The overall strength of relationships is measured through Total Link Strength (TLS), which captures the degree of integration of nodes within the network and allows this dimension to be distinguished from citation impact (Aria & Cuccurullo, 2017).

Within the fields of economics and management, this approach serves a meta-analytical function, enabling the identification of research domains, theoretical convergences, and marginal areas, and providing an empirical basis for the development of the theoretical framework and the identification of the research gap. However, these maps represent structures of proximity rather than causal relationships, and their interpretation remains inherently theoretical. Accordingly, the analysis is employed as a heuristic device, complemented by a critical reading of the literature, in order to ensure methodological rigor and interpretative robustness.

4 Results and Initial Evaluations

4.1 Publications Identified in Scopus

The Scopus search is therefore based on a query combining terms related to diaspora, investment, and entrepreneurship. Applying the search string to titles, abstracts, and keywords yields 1,886 documents, of which 667 fall within the Business, Management and Accounting subject area.

To enhance relevance to the research objective, the analysis is subsequently restricted to titles only, identifying 67 contributions, of which 45 belong to the Business, Management and Accounting area and 29 to Economics, Econometrics and Finance. Given the overlap between subject areas, the final dataset used for the analysis consists of 50 documents.

Figure 1 presents the main characteristics of the selected documents.

The temporal distribution of the documents reveals recent growth, largely concentrated in the past decade. The topic has therefore developed later than other areas within entrepreneurial finance, suggesting a research stream that remains in formation and lacks a consolidated theoretical tradition.

The geographical distribution shows a strong concentration in a limited number of countries, with a predominance of advanced academic contexts and increasing attention to emerging economies. This reflects the transnational nature of the phenomenon, but also points to a potential asymmetry between locations of scientific production and the empirical contexts under investigation.

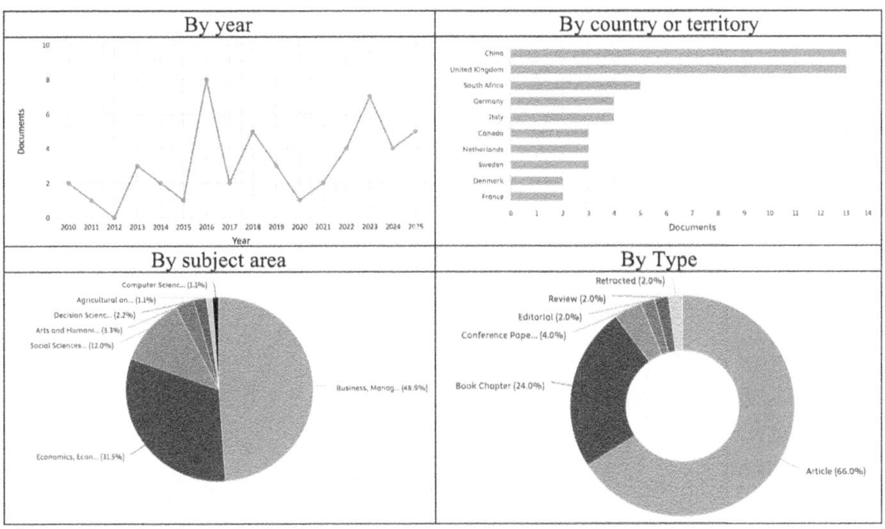

Fig. 1 Documents

The distribution by subject area and document type confirms the interdisciplinary nature of the field and the predominance of empirical contributions, further highlighting the absence of a consolidated theoretical framework.

Overall, the preliminary evidence points to a young, fragmented, and expanding field, characterized by increasing relevance but still lacking theoretical consolidation. This configuration supports the use of bibliometric tools and underscores the need for a systematic structuring of research streams.

4.2 *Bibliometric Mappings with VOSviewer*

4.2.1 The Documents

The 50 documents, of which only three are connected, are mapped in Fig. 2. Table 1, by contrast, reports the most relevant contributions.

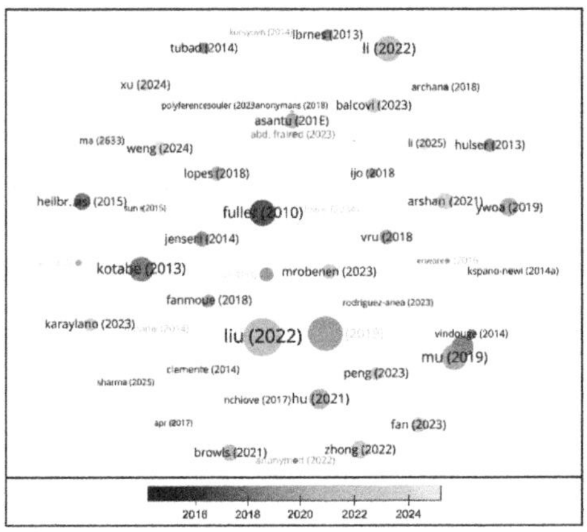

Fig. 2 The 50 documents. *Source* Authors' own elaboration

Table 1 Documents

With at least 35 citations			With at least 1 link		
Document	Cit	Links	Document	Cit	Links
Liu et al. (2022)	99	0	Tolciu (2011)	32	2
Williams and Krasniqi (2018)	79	0	Asante (2018)	15	2
Li et al. (2022)	44	0	Ma et al. (2019)	43	1
Ma et al. (2019)	43	1	Roskruge et al. (2016)	6	1
Fuller (2010)	43	0	Abd Hamid and Everett (2023)	4	1
Kotabe et al. (2013)	38	0	Anonymous (2018)	0	1

Source Authors' own elaboration

The analysis reveals a very weak relational structure within the dataset. The presence of only three links indicates a low level of cumulative integration in the literature. The most highly cited studies appear isolated from one another, suggesting that citation impact does not translate into structural centrality. By contrast, the few documents that are connected perform a bridging function, despite exhibiting lower citation counts. The findings confirm that the field is characterized by a strong capacity to mobilize capital, but a limited ability to structure investment processes. This misalignment between citations and connections points to a domain shaped by influential contributions that are not integrated into a cumulative scholarly debate.

The low network density further confirms that diaspora angel investing does not yet constitute an autonomous domain, but rather remains an intersection between migration, entrepreneurship, and finance studies.

4.2.2 The Authors

The analysis of authors confirms the weak structuring of the field at the scientific level. Out of 112 authors, only eight are connected through relational ties, indicating an extremely sparse network (Fig. 3 and Table 2).

In terms of network integration (TLS), Andreia Tolciu records the highest value (TLS = 7), with a single contribution and 32 citations, followed by Kofi Takyi Asante (TLS = 2, one document, 15 citations). All other authors display TLS values of 1.

The distribution of citations highlights a number of high-impact contributions that lack significant network connections (with TLS equal to or close to zero). By contrast, authors with higher levels of integration, such as Tolciu and Asante, exhibit lower citation counts but play a more central role within the network structure.

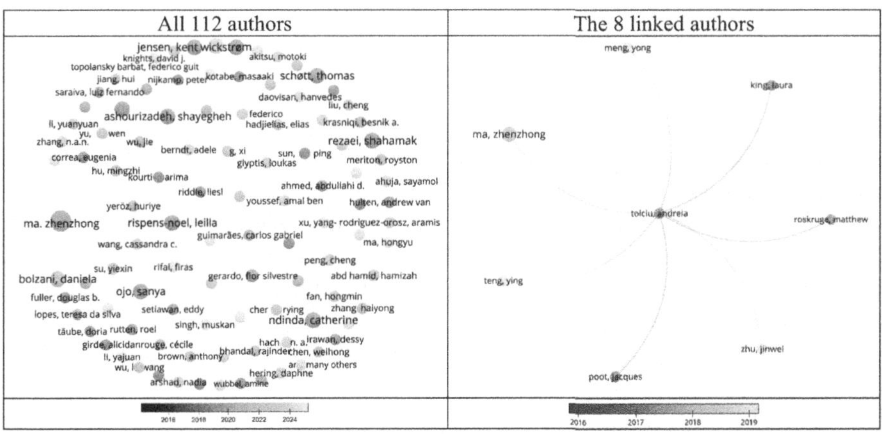

Fig. 3 The Authors. *Source* Authors' elaboration using VOSviewer

Table 2 Authors

With at least two publications				With at least 40 citations			
Author	Documents	Citations	TLS	Author	Documents	Citations	TLS
Ashourizadeh, Shayegheh	2	28	0	Chen, Xiuying	1	99	0
Bolzani, Daniela	2	21	0	Koster, Sierdjan	1	99	0
Jensen, Kent Wickstrøm	2	28	0	Liu, Sheng	1	99	0
Karayianni, Eva	2	11	0	Krasniqi, Besnik A	1	79	0
Ma, Zhenzhong	2	52	1	Williams, Nick	1	79	0
Ndhlovu, Tidings P	2	2	0	Ma, Zhenzhong	2	52	1
Ndinda, Catherine	2	2	0	Li, Yuanyuan	1	44	0
Ojo, Sanya	2	3	0	Tan, Jing	1	44	0
Opiniano, Jeremaiah M	2	1	0	Wu, Binyang	1	44	0
Rezaei, Shahamak	2	28	0	Yu, Jingwen	1	44	0
Rispens-Noel, Leila	2	1	0	Fuller, Douglas B	1	43	0
Schøtt, Thomas	2	28	0	Meng, Yong	1	43	1
				Teng, Ying	1	43	1
				Zhu, Jinwei	1	43	1

Source Authors' own elaboration

Overall, TLS values are generally low, predominantly equal to 0 or 1, with only a few exceptions, indicating limited interdependence among scholars and the absence of consolidated research clusters.

Taken together, the field is characterized by individual contributions or small, isolated groups rather than structured scientific communities. This reinforces the interpretation of a fragmented body of literature, still in an early stage of development and lacking clear theoretical cohesion.

4.2.3 Co-Authorship

Co-authorship captures collaborative relationships among authors, identifying who publishes with whom and, therefore, the social structure of scientific production.

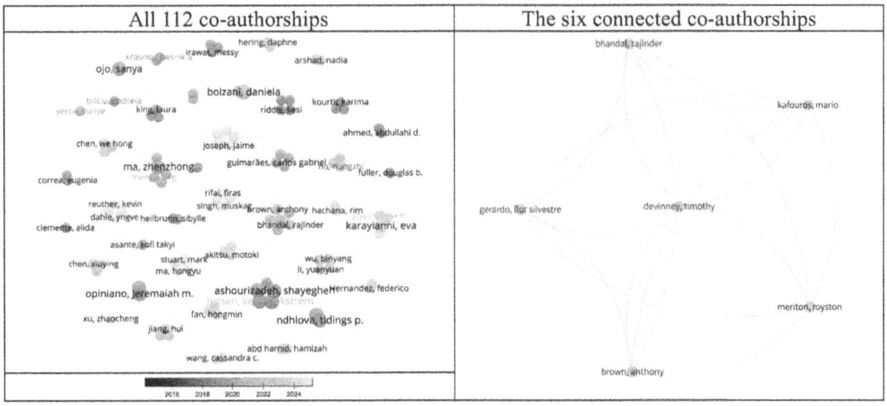

Fig. 4 Co-authorship networks. *Source* Authors' elaboration using VOSviewer

Unlike the citation links analysed above, which reflect cognitive and directional relationships between documents, co-authorship represents direct interactions among researchers, independent of citation mechanisms. This yields a complementary perspective: links inform the structure of the scholarly debate, whereas co-authorship sheds light on the formation of scientific communities.

Figure 4 depicts the overall network of collaborations among the 112 authors and the sub-network of those effectively connected (only six), while Table 3 summarizes the authors with the highest levels of productivity, impact, and relational integration.

TLS values associated with co-authorship are significantly higher than those observed in the citation networks reported in the previous table. This reflects the nature of the measure: in the case of co-authorship, TLS captures both the number and the intensity of direct collaborations, which tend to generate denser networks than citation-based relationships. As a result, authors with at least two publications may exhibit relatively high TLS values even in the absence of a corresponding citation impact.

The presence of a limited number of collaborative clusters with comparatively higher TLS, within an otherwise fragmented network, suggests that the field evolves through small research micro-clusters rather than consolidated scientific communities. The weak integration among authors reflects the absence of a shared framework on diaspora angel investing, consistent with the emerging nature of the topic and its dispersion across disciplinary domains. At the same time, the existence of these circumscribed collaborative networks points to potential poles of research development, which may contribute to the construction of more operational and systematic approaches, in line with the need for applicable tools and models.

Table 3 Co-authorships

With at least 2 publications				With at least 40 citations				With at least 4 TLS			
Author	Doc	Cit	TLS	Author	Doc	Cit	TLS	Author	Doc	Cit	TLS
Ashourizadeh, Shayegheh	2	28	7	Chen, Xiuying	1	99	2	Ashourizadeh, Shayegheh	2	28	7
Bolzani, Daniela	2	21	1	Koster, Sierdjan	1	99	2	Jensen, Kent Wickstrøm	2	28	7
Jensen, Kent Wickstrøm	2	28	7	Liu, Sheng	1	99	2	Rezaei, Shahamak	2	28	7
Karayianni, Eva	2	11	3	Krasniqi, Besnik A	1	79	1	Schøtt, Thomas	2	28	7
Ma, Zhenzhong	2	52	4	Williams, Nick	1	79	1	Bhandal, Rajinder	1	18	5
Ndhlovu, Tidings P	2	2	2	Ma, Zhenzhong	2	52	4	Brown, Anthony	1	18	5
Ndinda, Catherine	2	2	2	Li, Yuanyuan	1	44	3	Devinney, Timothy	1	18	5
Ojo, Sanya	2	3	0	Tan, Jing	1	44	3	Gerardo, Flor Silvestre	1	18	5
Opiniano, Jeremaiah M	2	1	2	Wu, Binyang	1	44	3	Kafouros, Mario	1	18	5
Rezaei, Shahamak	2	28	7	Yu, Jingwen	1	44	3	Meriton, Royston	1	18	5
Rispens-Noel, Leila	2	1	2	Fuller, Douglas B	1	43	0	Ma, Zhenzhong	2	52	4
Schøtt, Thomas	2	28	7	Meng, Yong	1	43	3	Li, Jizhen	1	15	4
				Teng, Ying	1	43	3	Joseph, Jaime	1	7	4
				Zhu, Jinwei	1	43	3	Knight, David W	1	7	4
								Li, Ping	1	7	4
								Li, Yajuan	1	7	4
								Xu, Yangyan	1	7	4

Source Authors' own elaboration

4.2.4 Keyword Co-Occurrence

Keyword co-occurrence measures the frequency with which two terms appear within the same documents, thereby enabling the identification of the conceptual structure of the field. Unlike citations and co-authorship, which reflect cognitive and social relationships, co-occurrence captures the semantic dimension of the literature.

Figure 5 depicts the keyword network (189 terms, of which 170 are connected).

The results indicate a concentration around a limited set of concepts, including entrepreneurship, China, social capital, and human capital. The centrality of social

Table 4 Keywords

With at least 3 occurrences			With at least TLS of at least 20		
Keyword	*Occurrences*	*TLS*	*Keyword*	*Occurrences*	*TLS*
Entrepreneurship	11	63	China	10	75
China	10	75	Entrepreneurship	11	63
Social Capital	9	57	Social Capital	9	57
Human Capital	8	42	Entrepreneur	5	52
Entrepreneur	5	52	Human Capital	8	42
Migrant Entrepreneurship	5	25	Immigrant	3	32
Entrepreneurs	4	20	Migration	4	31
Migration	4	31	Migrant Entrepreneurship	5	25
Community	3	12	Economic Development	2	22
Diaspora	3	21	Diaspora	3	21
Immigrant	3	32	Entrepreneurs	4	20

Source Authors' own elaboration

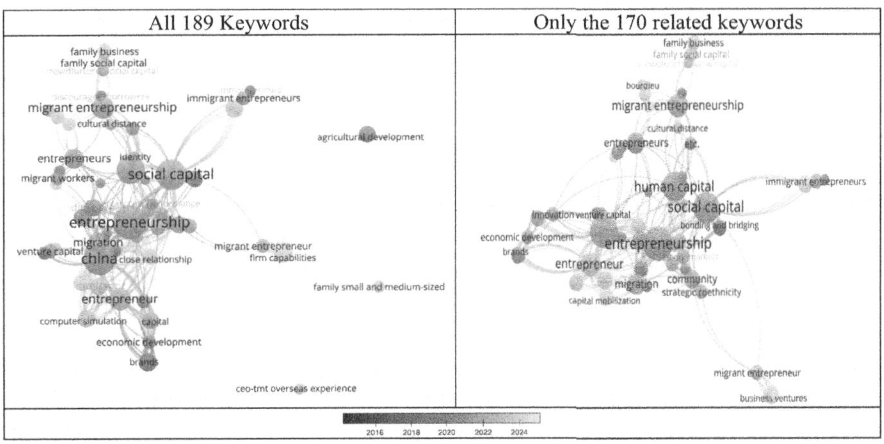

Fig. 5 Keywords. *Source* Authors' elaboration using VOSviewer

and human capital points to a predominantly socio-relational perspective. Migration-related terms further confirm the overlap with the corresponding body of literature.

Diaspora itself exhibits limited weight, as do financial terms such as angel investing and venture capital, indicating a weak focus on the investor side.

The field therefore appears to be dominated by entrepreneurial and sociological perspectives, with limited financial integration. A clear gap emerges, namely

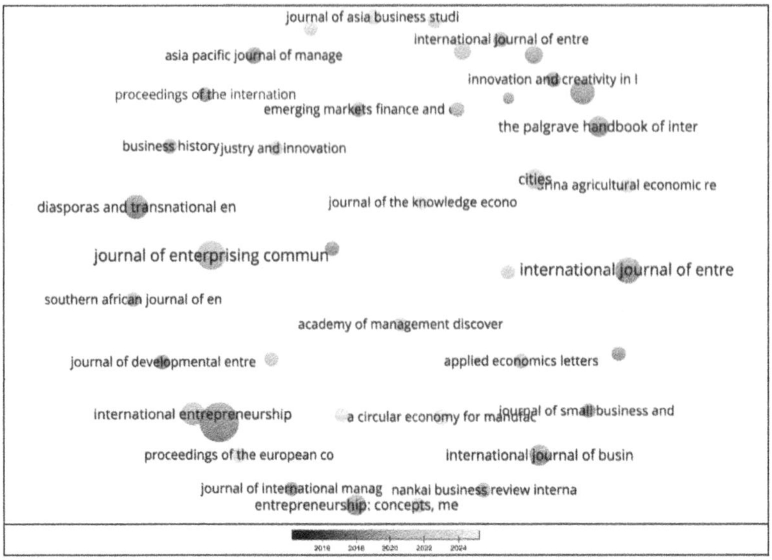

Fig. 6 All 38 sources. *Source* Authors' elaboration using VOSviewer

the absence of models and instruments for the operational mobilization of diaspora capital.

4.2.5 The Sources

The source analysis examines the distribution of publications across journals in order to identify potential core outlets. Figure 6 presents the full set of 38 sources, while Table 5 reports those with the highest levels of productivity and impact.

The results show an absence of relationships in terms of both citation links and bibliographic coupling (with TLS equal to zero), indicating complete editorial dispersion. Even the most frequently occurring journals do not form a consolidated core. This indicates that the field has not yet become institutionalized within a set of dedicated publication outlets, but rather dispersed across journals in entrepreneurship, management, and migration studies.

The fragmentation of sources is consistent with previous findings, namely the absence of cohesive scientific communities, weak theoretical integration, and the centrality of isolated contributions. This reinforces a key point, the lack of a consolidated tradition on diaspora angel investing as an autonomous domain. Consequently, there is scope for contributions that systematize the field and orient it toward more operational and financial dimensions.

Table 5 Sources

With at least 2 documents				With at least 30 citations			
Source	Doc	Cit	TLS	Source	Doc	Cit	TLS
Journal Of Enterprising Communities	4	47	1	Cities	2	112	0
International Journal of Entrepreneurial Behaviour and Research	3	96	1	International Journal of Entrepreneurial Behaviour and Research	3	96	1
Cities	2	112	0	Journal of International Entrepreneurship	1	79	0
Diasporas and Transnational Entrepreneurship in Global Contexts	2	4	0	Journal of Enterprising Communities	4	47	1
Entrepreneurship: Concepts, Methodologies, Tools, and Applications	2	1	0	Applied Economics Letters	1	44	0
Handbook of Social Capital and Regional Development	2	6	1	Asia Pacific Journal of Management	1	43	0
International Entrepreneurship and Management Journal	2	32	0	Journal of International Management	1	38	0
International Journal of Business and Globalisation	2	28	0	International Entrepreneurship and Management Journal	2	32	0
The Palgrave Handbook of International Labour Migration: Law and Policy Perspectives	2	1	0				

Source Authors' own elaboration

4.3 Dominant Thematic Areas

The review of the most relevant contributions identifies four dominant thematic areas.

The first concerns migrant and diaspora entrepreneurship, in which the diaspora is primarily analysed as a relational, identity-based, and reputational resource. Within this perspective, studies on migrant and transnational entrepreneurship interpret social capital, trust, embeddedness, and ethnic networks as mechanisms capable of reducing informational asymmetries and barriers to market access (Asante, 2018; Tolciu, 2011; Williams & Krasniqi, 2018). This stream provides a theoretical basis for understanding deal-sourcing, trust proxies, and the informal selection of opportunities.

The second area focuses on human capital, knowledge, and skills transfer. Here, the diaspora acts not only as an investor, but also as a conduit for managerial, technological, and institutional knowledge between the country of residence and the country of origin (Fuller, 2010; Kotabe et al., 2013; Liu et al., 2022). This stream clarifies the non-financial value of diaspora investment, yet remains weak in the formalization of operational instruments, such as term sheets, valuation practices, investment governance, and exit mechanisms, which are rarely addressed in a systematic manner.

The third area is geographical and institutional. The prominence of China and other emerging economies indicates that the phenomenon is primarily examined in contexts characterized by informational imperfections, less developed financial markets, and a strong reliance on transnational networks (Ma et al., 2019; Li et al., 2022). This stream is particularly relevant as it highlights where diaspora capital may compensate for institutional and financial constraints. However, it tends to prioritize contextual description over the development of country dashboards, sectoral benchmarks, or comparative metrics.

The fourth area, and the most underdeveloped, concerns entrepreneurial finance in the strict sense. Terms such as angel investing, venture capital, syndication, SPVs, valuation, diaspora bonds, and ESG remain marginal or absent. This reveals a clear gap, the literature explains why diaspora networks can mobilize capital, but provides far less insight into how such capital is structured, valued, contracted, and monitored. This constitutes the main research gap of the chapter, diaspora angel investing emerges more as a socio-entrepreneurial phenomenon than as a mature domain within entrepreneurial finance.

Overall, the most robust literature provides a coherent yet incomplete picture. The strongest contributions explain networks, trust, social capital, human capital, and transnational embeddedness, yet lack investor-side models capable of translating these resources into replicable investment instruments. This chapter seeks to address this gap by systematizing a fragmented field and demonstrating that future research should move from the description of diaspora networks toward the design of financial, contractual, and valuation mechanisms for the scalable mobilization of diaspora capital.

5 Discussion and Conclusions

The results allow for a coherent response to the research questions, highlighting a configuration of the field that remains fragile at both the theoretical and relational levels. With regard to RQ1, the intellectual structure of the literature appears weakly integrated, the limited density of citation links, the low cohesion among authors, and the absence of consolidated clusters point to a non-cumulative domain, characterized more by isolated contributions than by shared research trajectories. This evidence aligns with broader patterns documented in the literature on SME internationalization and entrepreneurship, where theoretical fragmentation represents a recurring condition (Dabić et al., 2020).

With reference to RQ2, the combined analysis of bibliometric mapping and systematic review reveals a clear predominance of approaches centred on social capital, human capital, and migrant entrepreneurship. The field develops around interpretative categories such as networks, trust, and embeddedness, which effectively explain mechanisms of resource access and opportunity identification, but are less suited to capturing the financial dimension of investment. This configuration is consistent with findings from major bibliometric analyses, which identify social capital, minority entrepreneurship, and network analysis as the dominant themes in the debate (Chhabra et al., 2022; Kumar et al., 2021).

RQ3 yields a particularly clear outcome. The existing literature does not yet allow diaspora angel investing to be conceptualized as an autonomous domain within entrepreneurial finance. While the factors enabling the mobilization of diaspora capital are well documented, there is a lack of systematic treatment of the mechanisms through which such capital is structured, valued, and governed, even in studies addressing transnational networks and institutional contexts (Fuller, 2010). Similarly, contributions examining transnational networks and institutional environments, despite recognizing the relevance of investment strategies and regulatory constraints, do not arrive at an operational formalization of financial processes.

Core early-stage investment instruments, such as syndication, investment vehicles, valuation models, and ESG criteria, remain marginal or absent. This reveals a gap with respect to investor-side approaches aimed at formalizing investment processes. This discrepancy between the mobilization of capital and its structuring constitutes the central interpretative contribution of the chapter. The literature explains the conditions under which investment emerges, but fails to develop models capable of rendering it replicable and scalable.

The theoretical implications point to the need to integrate socio-relational and financial perspectives, translating diaspora networks into operational investment mechanisms such as deal-sourcing, valuation practices, and the structuring of financial vehicles. From an operational standpoint, the findings suggest the urgency of transforming the relational resources of diasporas into formalized instruments capable of supporting investment selection, evaluation, and governance processes. In particular, trust, often treated as an informal mechanism, requires progressive institutionalization into due diligence practices, while diaspora networks may provide the foundation for syndication structures and transnational investment vehicles. These developments are especially relevant in contexts characterized by institutional and financial constraints, where diaspora capital can play a compensatory role.

The limitations of the chapter stem from the choice of database, which introduces unavoidable coverage biases, and from the size of the dataset, which reflects the nascent stage of the field rather than a methodological restriction. Moreover, the bibliometric nature of the analysis allows for the observation of relational and thematic structures, but does not permit causal inference, thus requiring integration with theoretical and, in future, empirical analyses.

Future research directions emerge clearly from the findings. There is a need to develop valuation models for investments in contexts characterized by high informational uncertainty, to analyse syndication dynamics among diaspora investors, to further explore innovative instruments such as diaspora bonds and impact vehicles, and to construct comparative metrics across countries and sectors. This transition, from a network-based perspective to an investor-side framework, represents a necessary condition for the theoretical and empirical maturation of the field.

References

Abd Hamid, H., & Everett, A. M. (2023). Migration contexts in shaping community ethnic resources: A forms of capital approach on ethnic migrant entrepreneurs in Malaysia. *Journal of Enterprising Communities: People and Places in the Global Economy, 17*(4), 834–855. https://doi.org/10.1108/JEC-09-2021-0139

Anonymous. (2018). Entrepreneurial strategies in deploying social capital: Exploring the art of strategic coethnicity in two Ghanaian migrant businesses. *Strategic Direction, 34*(12), 20–22. https://doi.org/10.1108/SD-10-2018-0203

Aria, M., & Cuccurullo, C. (2017). Bibliometrix: An R-tool for comprehensive science mapping analysis. *Journal of Informetrics, 11*(4), 959–975. https://doi.org/10.1016/j.joi.2017.08.007

Asante, K. T. (2018). Strategic coethnicity: Social capital and entrepreneurial strategies of two Ghanaian migrant businesses. *Journal of Enterprising Communities: People and Places in the Global Economy, 12*(4), 418–436. https://doi.org/10.1108/JEC-04-2017-0026

Chhabra, M., Dana, L.-P., Ramadani, V., & Agarwal, M. (2022). A retrospective overview of journal of enterprising communities: People and places in the global economy from 2007 to 2021 using a bibliometric analysis. *Journal of Enterprising Communities: People and Places in the Global Economy, 16*(6), 1051–1075. https://doi.org/10.1108/JEC-06-2021-0091

Dabić, M., Maley, J., Dana, L.-P., Novak, I., Pellegrini, M. M., & Caputo, A. (2020). Pathways of SME internationalization: A bibliometric and systematic review. *Small Business Economics, 55*(3), 705–725. https://doi.org/10.1007/s11187-019-00181-6

Donthu, N., Kumar, S., Mukherjee, D., Pandey, N., & Lim, W. M. (2021). How to conduct a bibliometric analysis: An overview and guidelines. *Journal of Business Research, 133*, 285–296. https://doi.org/10.1016/j.jbusres.2021.04.070

Drori, I., Honig, B., & Wright, M. (2009). Transnational entrepreneurship: An emergent field of study. *Entrepreneurship Theory and Practice, 33*(5), 1001–1022. https://doi.org/10.1111/j.1540-6520.2009.00332.x

Fuller, D. B. (2010). How law, politics and transnational networks affect technology entrepreneurship: Explaining divergent venture capital investing strategies in China. *Asia Pacific Journal of Management, 27*(3), 445–459. https://doi.org/10.1007/s10490-009-9149-0

Haq, M., & Yasin, N. (2025). Qualitative, quantitative, and mixed methodology paradigms. *Journal of Practical Studies in Education, 6*(6), 15–29.

Karayianni, E., Hadjielias, E., & Glyptis, L. (2023). Family across borders social capital and diaspora entrepreneurial preparedness. *Journal of Enterprising Communities: People and Places in the Global Economy, 17*(1), 46–71. https://doi.org/10.1108/JEC-03-2020-0030

Kotabe, M., Riddle, L., Sonderegger, P., & Täube, F. A. (2013). Diaspora investment and entrepreneurship: The role of people, their movements, and capital in the international economy. *Journal of International Management, 19*(1), 3–5. https://doi.org/10.1016/j.intman.2012.12.001

Kumar, S., Vanevenhoven, J., Liguori, E., Dana, L.-P., & Pandey, N. (2021). Twenty-five years of the *Journal of Small Business and Enterprise Development*: A bibliometric review. *Journal of Small Business and Enterprise Development, 28*(3), 429–455. https://doi.org/10.1108/JSBED-12-2020-0443

Li, Y., Tan, J., Wu, B., & Yu, J. (2022). Does digital finance promote entrepreneurship of migrants? Evidence from China. *Applied Economics Letters, 29*(19), 1829–1832. https://doi.org/10.1080/13504851.2021.1963404

Liu, S., Koster, S., & Chen, X. (2022). Digital divide or dividend? The impact of digital finance on migrants' entrepreneurship in less developed regions of China. *Cities, 131*, Article 103896. https://doi.org/10.1016/j.cities.2022.103896

Ma, Z., Zhu, J., Meng, Y., & Teng, Y. (2019). The impact of overseas human capital and social ties on Chinese returnee entrepreneurs' venture performance. *International Journal of Entrepreneurial Behaviour and Research, 25*(1), 67–83. https://doi.org/10.1108/IJEBR-07-2017-0246

Riddle, L., Hrivnak, G. A., & Nielsen, T. M. (2010). Transnational diaspora entrepreneurship in emerging markets: Bridging institutional divides. *Journal of International Management, 16*(4), 398–411. https://doi.org/10.1016/j.intman.2010.09.009

Roskruge, M., Poot, J., & King, L. (2016). Social capital, entrepreneurship and living standards: Differences between migrants and the native born. In H. Westlund & J. P. Larsson (Eds.), *Handbook of social capital and regional development* (pp. 221–254). Edward Elgar Publishing.

Saxenian, A. (2005). From brain drain to brain circulation: Transnational communities and regional upgrading in India and China. *Studies in Comparative International Development, 40*(2), 35–61. https://doi.org/10.1007/BF02686293

Tolciu, A. (2011). Migrant entrepreneurs and social capital: A revised perspective. *International Journal of Entrepreneurial Behaviour and Research, 17*(4), 409–427. https://doi.org/10.1108/13552551111139647

Tranfield, D., Denyer, D., & Smart, P. (2003). Towards a methodology for developing evidence-informed management knowledge by means of systematic review. *British Journal of Management, 14*(3), 207–222. https://doi.org/10.1111/1467-8551.00375

Van Eck, N. J., & Waltman, L. (2010). Software survey: VOSviewer, a computer program for bibliometric mapping. *Scientometrics, 84*(2), 523–538. https://doi.org/10.1007/s11192-009-0146-3

Van Eck, N. J., & Waltman, L. (2014). Visualizing bibliometric networks. In Y. Ding, R. Rousseau, & D. Wolfram (Eds.), *Measuring scholarly impact* (pp. 285–320). Springer. https://doi.org/10.1007/978-3-319-10377-8_13

Williams, N., & Krasniqi, B. A. (2018). Coming out of conflict: How migrant entrepreneurs utilise human and social capital. *Journal of International Entrepreneurship, 16*(2), 301–323. https://doi.org/10.1007/s10843-017-0221-4

Wu, J., & Ma, Z. (2018). Misfit or xenophilia: The impact of overseas work experiences on returnee entrepreneurs' venture capital funding in China. *Nankai Business Review International, 9*(1), 19–32. https://doi.org/10.1108/NBRI-06-2015-0016

Zupic, I., & Čater, T. (2015). Bibliometric methods in management and organization. *Organizational Research Methods, 18*(3), 429–472. https://doi.org/10.1177/1094428114562629

Yasin, N. (2022). Cold grass or hot sands: A comparative study of immigrant Punjabi-Pakistani entrepreneurs in London and Dubai. *Strategic Change: Briefings in Entrepreneurial Finance., 31*(4), 1–10.

Yasin, N., & Hafeez, K. (2023). Three waves of immigrant entrepreneurship. A cross-national comparative study. *Small Business Economics: An Entrepreneurship Journal, 60*(1), 1281–1306 https://doi.org/10.1007/s11187-022-0065z

Yasin, N., Haq, M., Hafeez, K., & Zahoor, N. (2025). Are some immigrant entrepreneurs more privileged than others? A cross-national comparison of financial capital among start-ups in the UK and UAE. *The Journal of Race, Ethnicity, and Politics*, 1–24. https://doi.org/10.1017/rep.2025.10031

Yasin, N., Hafeez, K., & Salamzadeh, A. (2024). A cross-country comparative ethnographic analysis of immigrant enclave entrepreneurship. *Qualitative Market Research: An International Journal, 28*(1), 1–37. https://doi.org/10.1108/QMR-11-2023-0164

The manufacturer's authorised representative in the EU is Springer Nature Customer Service Centre GmbH, Europaplatz 3, 69115 Heidelberg, Germany. If you have any concerns regarding our products, please contact ProductSafety@springernature.com

Printed and bound by CPI Group (UK) Ltd, Croydon, CR0 4YY
16/09/2026
02217795-0003